DRUG CONSPIRACY

DRUG CONSPIRACY

'We Only Want the Blacks' — My Persecution by the United States Government

BY

RICHARD 'SQUIRREL' THOMAS

PUBLISHED FOR

CRESCENDO MEDIA WORKS, LLC
BIRMINGHAM

BY NEWSOUTH BOOKS
MONTGOMERY

Crescendo Media Works, LLC
P.O. Box 360194
Birmingham, Alabama 35236
www.crescendomediaworks.com

Library of Congress Cataloging-in-Publication Data

Thomas, Richard, 1942 Jan. 16–
Drug conspiracy : we only want the Blacks : my persecution by the United States government
/ by Richard "Squirrel" Thomas.
p. cm.
Includes bibliographical references and index.

ISBN-13: 978-1-60306-064-6 (alk. paper)
ISBN-10: 1-60306-064-2 (alk. paper)
ISBN-13: 978-1-60306-065-3 (ebook)

1. Drug traffic—Alabama—Prevention. 2. Discrimination in law enforcement—Alabama.
3. Race discrimination—Alabama. 4. Thomas, Richard, 1942 Jan. 16– I. Title.
HV8079.N3T46 2011
364.1'77092—dc22
[B]

2010047907

Front cover images © iStockphoto.com/Spauln (top)/mgkaya (bottom)

Book design by Randall Williams

Printed in the United States of America

To my brother, the late John R. Thomas, retired Agent
with the United States Department of the Interior;

To the late Judge Charles S. Conley;
the late Urelee Earl Gordon, Sr.; Raymond Cohen;
Rhoderick D. D. Dickerson; the late Gaston Bell;
the late Albert "Bones" Mitchell; Frank Armstead;
Alonzo R. Seymour;

And to Willie Mae Whitlow, Civil Rights Activist
and Teacher, who suggested I write this book
to tell the world.

Contents

INTRODUCTION

In the criminal justice system, filled with rogue prosecutors, police officers who take money from drug suspects without reporting it, attorneys who receive drug proceeds, selective prosecution based on race and class, and convicted felons who falsely testify against the innocent in exchange for the POSSIBILITY of being granted a reduced sentence—nineteen men were arrested and sentenced in a high profile case involving the sell and distribution of millions of dollars of cocaine in the Middle District of Alabama. One of those men was Richard "Squirrel" Thomas of Montgomery, Alabama. Now that judgment has been passed through media, mouth, and mind, there is indeed a truth to it all. The *Montgomery Advertiser*, Channel 12, and the U.S. Attorney's office conspired knowingly or unknowingly to ruin my business and my name, resulting in my loss of more than a million dollars. This is my story.

Prologue: February 16, 1994

On February 16, 1994, on the last day of my normal life—before the nightmare began, before federal agents came into my house and raided my safe, before the dogged dark decade of endless harassment—I visited Atlanta, Georgia. I shaved and showered, I dressed, I ate breakfast, all with an invisible noose hanging above my head.

Unknown to me at the time, my name had come across someone's desk. I, Richard "Squirrel" Thomas, retired math teacher and business owner, was about to become another victim in the American War on Drugs. The subsequent fallout defamed my character, wrecked my business, and ruined my life.

I had planned out my day in the largest city in the Deep South. The day was cloudy and cool when I got into my car with my good friend, Ed Mastin, and got onto I-85. In Atlanta, the roads were crowded with mid-morning traffic. We took the International Boulevard exit to Spring Street and parked in the deck. At last we reached our destination, the Apparel Mart. We were there to repair my friend Helen Frustick's computer and do a little shopping on the side. We chatted about things and looked through the aisles of clothes. I walked along without a care in the world. What did I have to worry about? Then I received a phone call.

The word conspiracy may be defined as an agreement among conspirators to plan secretly an unlawful act or plot. A drug conspiracy, in my view, would be defined as an agreement among conspirators to plan secretly unlawful acts pertaining to the sale or distribution of illegal drugs. Those involved, breaking the law, should be punished. But what does it say about the integrity of the American justice system when the guilty are set free and the innocent are put in chains?

The phone call was from a friend, explaining that back in Montgomery the police and DEA were all around the business of an acquaintance of mine, Curtis Drayton, on Carter Hill Road. Other agents were active on Vaughn Road at the house of Marie Thomas, Curtis Drayton's girlfriend. Weird, I thought. In short order I got another call from another friend. The DEA were now at Curtis's house in Prattville. I asked what was going on and he didn't know, but the police, FBI and DEA were swarmed around all three places.

I have to question the motives of the drug war. Who benefits? The war has spilled over into numerous other countries: Colombia, Mexico, the Middle East. Scores of people are incarcerated every year from infractions involving the drug policies. The drug problem isn't going away. In fact, it appears to be getting worse. And, meanwhile, a lot of innocent people are being hurt. In my case, I wonder about the integrity and ethics of the associates of the criminal justice system of the Middle District of Alabama.

As I later navigated the corridors of the United States District Court System, I was awed by the shamelessness with which the manipulative system crushed the innocent and guilty alike, selectively passing over some suspects for a variety of reasons, mostly centering on their wealth and status in middle-class society.

I'm hoping that telling my story might help change a corrupt and racist apparatus that has ruined thousands of lives. At the moment, I have no trust or confidence in the criminal justice system. I've experienced too much. My life is a prime example of how the system can and will manipulate, misrepresent, discriminate, and prosecute blacks and poor whites regardless of their innocence or the evidence. I'm hoping that things can change. I'm hoping that the innocent black man incarcerated today might not have to experience what I've gone through. I know hope isn't enough.

What follows is one man's run-in with a vast, vicious bureaucratic system. It's a David-versus-Goliath story without the fairy tale ending. For however my life ends up, however I recover from the more than decade-long odyssey, the system remains in place. Ultimately I dodged the bullet, but thousands of others wait to take the hit. The nightmare remains, it never sleeps, it has no remorse, and unless some major changes occur within both the criminal justice system and society at large, it will never go away.

This is the story of a time, a place, a people, and a legal system. But this is also the story of my life. For I am more than just a victim. The decisions I made throughout my life, all in accordance with the law, resulted in my arrest. The story details how I began my career as a gambler, as a teacher, and a nightclub owner. It follows me through my young hustling years to middle-age. I probably won't write another book. And although it is the crimes against me and others like me that propelled me to write this in the first place, I feel that in the process I should tell the rest of the story.

Most of this book is comprised of facts and is a matter of public record. My opinions will be obvious. But most of this book is culled from court reports. So if you have a problem with some of the things said in this book, blame the court reporter. I sometimes use rough language in the telling. Well, if I have to choose between bad words, bad people, or bad ideas, I'll take the bad language every time. At my age, I say what I mean and what I feel. I speak the truth, in all its ugly and beautiful forms.

THE CITY OF MONTGOMERY, after the eight-lane interstates of Atlanta and the gridlock traffic, was a welcome sight as Ed and I returned home that night. I went to my club. I was playing records during happy hour when James Gosha, an acquaintance, came in.

"I heard about the arrests," I said.

"Squirrel," he said, "all hell has broken loose. They have arrested all the boys."

"Why?"

"Well, you know they took three keys from Curtis on Super Bowl Sunday."

"What's a key?" I asked.

He looked at me and left. I kept playing records and when happy hour was over, I left the club with some poker-playing friends and went to the shoe shop to play poker as we normally did. We played poker all night. During the game, I got a call from Wallace Salery from the Elmore County Jail. Wallace had been in jail two or three years. He said my name was on a complaint and that I was going to be picked up. I wrote it off, thinking he was mistaken.

"The complaint says 'conspiracy to distribute cocaine in the Middle District of Alabama,'" he said.

"Man, I don't know anything about any damn cocaine!"

"I know you don't," he said, "but they are going to pick you up. Your name is on the complaint."

I thought about things for a moment, the sounds of the game behind me. Maybe they didn't pick me up earlier because I was in Atlanta, and maybe they were looking for me right now. I knew I was innocent, though, and that everything would work out. I wasn't worried. I hadn't done a single thing wrong.

When the game broke up, one guy noticed police cars up the street, the chrome shining under the orange glow of the street lamps, the emergency lights still and quiet.

"I'm glad they are watching because it makes me feel safer," I said. "I'd rather them fine me fifteen dollars for gambling than for one of the fools to put a pistol in my head." My buddies laughed and went on their way. We all should have known better: a black man in the Heart of Dixie can have only so much trust in the law.

I went home around midnight and sat with my feet up in a big old comfortable chair. Then I got in bed and I fell asleep. And when I woke up the next morning, my life was destroyed.

THE EARLY YEARS

I was born Friday, January 16, 1942. My mother recounts my arrival on game night while Alabama State was playing Tuskegee Institute in basketball. The third child of Dimple Mae Thomas and Hiawatha Thomas, I began my early education among several recognized names of Montgomery, Alabama. I started nursery school at Alabama State College (now Alabama State University) in the basement of Beverly Hall. My twenty-five classmates included Stephen James, Craig Beverly, Betty Jean Gordon, and Harper Council Trenholm, Jr., whose father was president of Alabama State. We attended nursery school, kindergarten, elementary school, and high school at Alabama State. As a teenager, I attended Alabama State Laboratory High School. Most of the twenty-five that started nursery school together were in the same high school graduating class. College professors taught the majority of our elective courses such as French, Spanish, Geometry, Chemistry, Latin, and Industrial Arts. My Industrial Arts teacher, Dr. Thomas Robinson, a Penn State University graduate, would later play a major role in my life. He taught me to be the best at what I do, to be trustworthy, to work hard every day, and to be a gentleman. I can hear him today saying, "Richie, we are not making a project for you to take home to your mother and she kiss you and say, 'You made this for me'—knowing she was going to put the piece of junk in the attic and forget about it. We are making projects to be sold to Haverty's or Bishop Parker Furniture stores." Dr. Robinson taught me woodworking skills and mechanical drawing. When you could correctly give him the front view, right side view, and top view of a pyramid tilted forty-five degrees, he thought you were a top gun.

My father, Hiawatha Thomas, was a shoe repairer and all his sons had to be able to fix shoes in his shoe shop at 553 South Jackson Street, near downtown Montgomery. It was a big day in our family when daddy pronounced one of his boys as a shoe repairer, at which time you were given tools, a jack, and a workbench in the shop. My brother John, two years younger than me, and I started at the tender ages of ten and eight as stockroom boys; we had to keep all the leather soles and rubber heels grouped together by sizes nine to ten, ten to eleven, eleven to twelve, and twelve to thirteen.

Daddy promoted me to shine boy at twelve years old. I remember shining shoes from 7 AM until 5 PM nonstop, without lunch, during the Alabama State Teachers Association meeting, which was held for black teachers at Alabama State College. Daddy believed in making money and that hard work kept you out of trouble and it also didn't allow you time to spend the money you had earned. He would say, "You rest when you die and that is a long, long rest." He taught me to save half the money I earned and give one-fourth to my mother, I kept one-fourth but even tried to save some of it. Saving money was a virtue unto itself. This, among other things, my father taught me.

At twelve I got a paper route delivering the afternoon *Alabama Journal*. I started with sixty-five papers and built my route to one hundred twenty papers. I chose a route near Alabama State's campus because I was very familiar with the area. I would come down Tuscaloosa Street throwing the homes and businesses of Dr. Hardy, the Nesbitts, the Johnsons, then down Jackson Street, throwing Campbell, Durite Cleaners, my father's shoe shop, up the hill and back down to Alabama State's campus to Abercrombie Hall, faculty circle, and Hamilton Street. I had great memories of Hamilton Street because I threw every house on that street and many of the elderly people had special requests like having their paper under a certain flowerpot or inside the screen door. I tried my best to make everybody on Hamilton Street happy by giving the service they wanted.

On Saturdays, once I left Hamilton Street I had over half of my paper bill collected because everyone on Hamilton Street paid me. I would then proceed to Carter Hill Road and I threw the right side to Mr. Spears's home and came down to Walnut Street throwing papers to the veterans in buildings V1, V2, V3, and V4 where the veterans coming out of Korea were housed while they attended Alabama State. I would then end up back at the paper house where I started. I learned to do this route in less than forty-five minutes.

Mr. Freddy Burke, a student at Alabama State and a member of Kappa Alpha Psi Fraternity, was my paper manager. He was another gentleman who later played a major role in my life. When I was fourteen my childhood friend Drake Ligon was a janitor at the Pilgrim Health & Life Insurance Company in downtown Montgomery on Monroe Street, next to Dean's Drug Store. When Drake began attending Alabama A&M in Huntsville, Alabama, he recommended me for the job. Mr. C. R. Williams was the president of the insurance company and Mr. Robert Nesbitt, Sr., was the district manager. I accepted and held the job until the day I graduated college, then passed it on to my brother, John. I never missed a day of work and was given the key to go in the building after hours. I recall playing basketball for Alabama State Lab and traveling out of town to play Alex City. On the way back, I would have the bus driver drop me off as close as he could and I would walk the rest of the way to Pilgrim Health & Life Insurance Company. I would work sometimes until 3 and 4 AM. This was during the time of segregation. I never had any problems late at night. The police officers knew me and continued to patrol.

So now I'm shining shoes at Hiawatha's Shoe Shop, I have a paper route, I'm fixing shoes, I'm a janitor at the insurance company, and I'm in charge of making and repairing fraternity paddles for Dr. Thomas Robinson at Alabama State's Industrial Arts department. Dr. Robinson would leave the department with me, a high school student, and the college students would have to get permission from me to work on their projects after school. Needless to say, it didn't go over too well with the college students watching a high school boy run the show. Yet Dr. Robinson trusted me and played a major role in my life.

A LOT HAS BEEN made of segregation in the South, how hard life could be, the constant belittling, the danger of stepping out of place when white folks were around. Montgomery was one of the most segregated cities in the South, and one of the most racist. It was, after all, called the Heart of Dixie.

We viewed whites with distrust. We saw the whites in charge as unfriendly at best, terrible and violent at worst. Every day we were reminded of our second-class citizenship.

There were some white people we respected, though: federal agents. My mother told me when I was going to Lundy's in 1962, "If you get into any kind of trouble, try to make it to a federal agent." She said once you get out of the South you'll be all right, but in the South try to make it to a federal agent. Federal agents were known in our communities as fairer than other white folks, more likely to listen to complaints, and more likely to help. Federal agents were, at least in comparison to the majority of other whites, the good guys. I want to stress this important point. I grew up thinking federal agents, and by proxy the federal government, were looking out for me in a way the state government and their agents—the police, local officials, and so on—were not. I held federal agents on a pedestal.

As I grew older I continued to work hard. You name the job—I had it. I completed high school in May 1960 and enrolled immediately in Alabama State in June 1960. I was in the class with the valedictorian and salutatorian of Booker T. Washington High School. I questioned the status of my college's English and public speaking curriculum because I was rated first in this class, yet I had been almost last in my high school class in English. I felt that Alabama State's English and public speaking classes must have been in bad shape. However, I was first in my high school class in mathematics and industrial arts. They were the two things I loved and the two things I fully concentrated on.

I WAS INTRODUCED TO gambling at a very young age. It started with a gentleman coming by my father's shoe shop to pick up bets from Daddy and his workers, then to Eli Café, Cabin Inn, the barber shop, then he would take a bus downtown to Mr. Boyd's place, who was a bookie. He would take all the bets to Mr. Boyd who paid him a commission for the number of bets he'd taken. This would be like clockwork every day. The person taking the bets would have the odds. For example, a person betting may have the opportunity to place a sixty-cent bet or a dollar twenty-cent bet. At twelve I witnessed these gentlemen give and receive bets and when I was around thirteen I began to do the same thing. I thought I would shine shoes a little harder to have extra money to support my gambling habit. If I hit I would buy nice shoes and clothes. My family lived about fifty yards from Jackson Davis Dormitory on Alabama State's campus. I spent my tenth- and eleventh-grade years gambling with college students almost every night. My brother John was very smart; his class included Levi Watkins, Jr., and Nicki Walton. Nicki became a skin specialist operating out of Birmingham and Montgomery, while Levi (attorney Donald Watkins's older brother) is one of the top open heart surgeons in the country. Levi also taught at Johns Hopkins University in Baltimore, Maryland. My brother John and these two gentlemen were geniuses. John had the highest score ever made on the federal entrance exam in Montgomery until 1965. He begged me to stop gambling in the dormitory at night with the college students and focus on my English deficiency. However, the college students couldn't gamble very well and didn't know the odds. Therefore it was just a matter of time before I would break them. The slick guys out of Birmingham who knew dice and cards recognized that I was sharp, too. We would give a hint that we were going to split what we made instead of playing against one another. We would rake in our winnings and split the profit after the game broke up.

Gambling fascinated me and I loved it. My principal, Mr. W. H. Coston, who later became the registrar at Alabama State, caught me gambling and told me that gambling would be my downfall. He stated, "You are going to win at gambling because you understand odds and probabilities but when you win at gambling nobody likes you; the guys you beat don't like you, the stick-up men don't like you, the IRS don't like you, and the police don't like you. But with a good brain you may be able to handle it."

I was always near a dice game. But I never touched the dice. All I wanted to do was fade the dice and place a bad bet. If the odds were eight to one, I would offer a guy a five to one bet. For instance, if a shooter thinks he can make an eight with two fours, I would pay him five to one. I would put a hundred against the shooter's twenty for a five-to-one bet. If he made two fours he would get the hundred. If he didn't, I would collect his twenty. These were still bad odds, made attractive by a high-dollar offer. This is the reason why it was just a matter of time before I would break my opponent.

The odds and probabilities aren't in their favor. The only exception was luck. Nothing beats luck.

A gambler is a different person altogether. A gambler wants the odds in his favor. For example, if a coin is flipped and there is a twenty-dollar bet the coin won't land on heads, I don't want the bet because the chance is fifty-fifty. When I bet, I want at least a sixty percent chance of winning. That is what gambling is all about. Some people list a guy as a gambler when he's really a fool. He is only a participating gambler. What is really beautiful is when a group of true gamblers come together and gamble. Everyone knows the proper odds and the winner is usually the lucky one in the bunch.

Later when I attended the white gambling games with the white bookies and the white bankers and lawyers, they all knew the proper odds. In the white game you would always find shooters. Everyone wanted to shoot. In the black game you would find mostly faders. A fader was the gambler that would bet you wouldn't make your point. This was big in the black dice game. Many aspiring gamblers didn't understand the true concept of gambling and odds. This was one of the main reasons why I never touched the dice. Because I understood probabilities and odds, I knew that it was just a matter of time before I raked the money off the table. Therefore, I didn't want the shooter to think I had switched the dice or loaded them.

Cheating was another hurdle in the black dice game. Cheaters would sometimes take the dice and boil them then press the six on one dice and the one on the other, therefore increasing the odds that a seven will be rolled. Or they could buy dice already set to do so. I attended a dice game one night at the Tuskegee Elks Club and the house man had a pair of preset dice. He would cut more because the dice were preset to crap. The odds were in his favor. I caught on to what was going on because I would always observe the game for thirty minutes before playing. I would then bet accordingly. I would then bet guys three to two that they couldn't roll a particular number. Many of them didn't like three to two therefore I would say, "Put down forty and pick up a hundred." They liked the sound of that better.

With the seed money from my various jobs, gambling was a very lucrative pastime for me. I gambled through all four years of college and for the rest of my life.

MY GODFATHER, GASTON BELL, was one of the most prominent figures in Montgomery. He gave me permission to gamble in Montgomery. He was respected, plugged in, and powerful. I remember when I was twenty-six getting a ticket for going the wrong way down a one-way street. I brought it to him and he immediately got on the phone and requested that the officer who issued the ticket come to see him.

Gaston said to me, "Squirrel, get you a Miller and a bologna sand-wich!"

So, I'm sitting up there eating a bologna sandwich and drinking a Miller beer. Here comes the white cop. Remember this is in 1968.

"This is my man Squirrel. Don't you ever give him a damn ticket again!" Gaston exclaimed to this white officer. I couldn't believe it. He said, "If you give him another ticket I'm going to take you out of that car and put you on foot, patrolling the Ritz Theatre on Monroe Street!"

He then took the ticket, tore it up, and threw it at the police. I couldn't believe it.

Another time, Gaston had a small fender bender with a black guy. When the police arrived, the man stated that Gaston hit him and drug his car down the street. Gaston jumped up and said, "I was going to try to help you because I did hit you, but now you are lying."

Gaston got back in his car, drove off, and left the black man and the police there. He was something else.

Another time, he sent me over to Delchamps to pick up a package for him. I asked for the butcher and he handed me a box filled with steaks, lamb chops, etc. I returned and said, "Mr. Bell, I've got your package. What do you want me to do with it?"

"Eat it, damn it! Don't you eat meat?" he loudly replied.

See, Bell was what people called the HNIC—the head nigger in charge. Back then, and now, too, although things have changed, there was an HNIC in every Southern town, especially small towns. A big, powerful black guy who got things done. Black people went to him for all problems. He ran the Bel-Air community, where my grandmother stayed.

People liked me when I was coming up. I kept my mouth shut and I didn't discuss anything. I kept my nose clean but I liked to gamble and I sometimes did little favors for some of the old-timers. I was one step ahead of the law, all the time. So Bell told the vice squad to leave me alone and let me gamble. And I did whatever he asked. Little errands. I would go to grocery stores and tell the owners that he sent me and they would fill up a box with beer and steaks. In a sense he introduced me into the world of gambling, the late-nighters, and the sometimes criminals. But I had nothing to do with that. I just liked cards and I liked making Bell happy, because when he was happy, I usually was, too.

I BEGAN COLLEGE IN the summer of 1960. I majored in elementary education, because of the need for men in elementary school, and minored in industrial arts. Dr. Robinson had taught industrial arts to me my seventh, ninth, eleventh, and twelfth-grade years. He had taught me all my life.

This was the era of the civil rights movement. Blacks all over the South were mobilizing, protesting. This was the era of the sit-in. This was the era of the Freedom Ride. The cultural landscape was changing. We could all feel it in the music, in the movie theaters, in the speeches we heard over the radio; this was the era of a nonviolent revolution. It was a dangerous time, a thrilling time.

It was a great time to be in college.

The spring of 1961 a friend of mine and I went to the Carver Theater looking for girls. They were not there and we were told that they were at First Baptist Church attending a rally for the Freedom Riders who had been beaten the day before at the Greyhound bus station. Dr. King and Reverend Abernathy and hundreds of people were inside the church. We rushed to the rally and then watched as the Ku Klux Klan surrounded the church. They yelled obscenities at us and threw rocks and tear gas into the church. The church had no air conditioning, so the tear gas floated along the floor with no ventilation.

I remember Dr. King calling President Kennedy and requesting that he activate the National Guard to come to the church and escort us safely home. I remember the National Guard trucks having designated markings on their sides that read Carver Park, Alabama State, North Montgomery and other destinations. My friend and I assisted the older ladies and made sure they got on the different army trucks. The *New York Times* and other media sources were on hand photographing the event. They photographed my friend, Julius Birch, and me helping the ladies onto the Army trucks in Montgomery, Alabama. Moments later Julius said to me, "We're not going to go through this all summer . . . let's go to New York."

Julius chose New York because his aunts and cousins lived in Harlem on 5th Avenue and 117th Street.

THAT SUMMER WE WENT by train to New York. From Atlanta to Washington to New York we rode. I recall the conductor's voice yelling at each point, "Philadelphia, Pennsylvania, Newark, New Jersey!"

After leaving Newark, moments later the train seemed to be on water. I looked out and there was seaweed sticking out of the water. Suddenly there was a gradual movement in the train that increased to top speed accompanied by an intense zooming sound. The lights went out and our ears tightened. Minutes later the conductor yelled, "Penn Station, New York, New York!!!"

I left the train, crossed the tracks, and went into Penn Station. We were at the bottom of Penn Station and had to take an escalator to the top. Julius, who had been to New York before, brought me outside to get a view of the city. I was amazed at the size of the buildings. They appeared to be a direct passage into the clouds. I marveled at the miles of steel and concrete. A boy from Alabama in 1961 had seen only so much.

We proceeded to the subway and rode into Harlem to his aunt's home. His aunt's daughter, Alma, let us in and told us that we would be occupying the front bedroom. Alma's boyfriend worked for Lundy Brothers Restaurant in Sheepheads Bay, Brooklyn, the third largest restaurant in the world. He told Julius that he would take him to work with him on the following Monday and get him a job as a waiter. Meanwhile, Alma's mother had gotten me a job across the street at the local grocery store where her boyfriend was the butcher. I assumed duties at the grocery store as a bag boy while taking on other tasks as they would arise. I cleaned the store—mopping and sweeping along with general tidying up.

Julius came home one night talking about the huge restaurant he worked in that served over three thousand people at one time while another thousand awaited seats. He said that he had already told the headwaiter that he had a buddy who wanted to work. They agreed to bring me out the following Sunday. That Sunday I arrived and the headwaiter hired me as a busboy. My job consisted of walking through the restaurant with a broom and dustpan with a handle attached and sweeping up trash and other debris. The headwaiter was impressed with my effort and the following Monday he made me a front man. The restaurant sat on Sheepshead Bay and as the people approached the restaurant on their boats they would come in the restaurant to get to-go orders. As a front man I had to take orders, receive them, bag the food up, and take them out to the boat. These people were very generous tippers.

I was promoted to a waiter after doing such a great job as a front man for two weeks. The headwaiter taught me how to carry the food. "You put it on the tray and forget about it and pretty soon you will learn how to grip the tray," he said.

I soon realized that I could average about $255 a night in tips alone. This was heaven to me. I compared it to my father who made $175 a week fixing shoes. I was in high cotton.

The waiter knew me as his can-to-can't man. He said I would work from when I can to when I can't. I never took a day off and had a goal of making $275 in tips a night. I soon became a head waiter. Only fifty waiters opened the first section of the clam bar from noon to 5 PM daily. I soon realized that most customers wanted clam chowder, clam broth, and biscuits. They were tipping fifty to seventy-five cents. Some of the waiters would say that they weren't going to waste their time waiting on those snakes. I saw this as an opportunity to get twelve bowls instead of two. I would tell the waiters to rest and talk about the baseball game and I'd handle their station. I would bring twelve bowls of clam chowder out which impressed the checkers and the owner's brother who was a manager. They would say I was a working fool because they would see me going in and out of the kitchen all day long getting orders.

During the day, I would try to make at least $75 in tips. I soon became a night waiter after 5 o'clock. The night waiters were very busy and would serve twelve to fourteen people. I carried fourteen people at night. I had very elaborate customers, many of them Italians. They appeared to be very wealthy. I told my customers to call me "Big Party Thomas." I would treat the ladies like royalty: pulling out their chairs, brushing the seats off, placing a menu before everyone and immediately going to the kitchen to get water and a plate of biscuits. I would then return, take orders—ladies first and provide them with the best service I possibly could. I would get tips of $35 to $40.

The cooks had specific duties. They had four men that broiled fish, four men that fried fish, two men that fried french fries, two that dipped vegetables, four that cooked lobster all day, four that broiled steak and chicken all day, two big guys that made 144 homemade biscuits at a time, and two dipped ice cream all day. In the middle of the kitchen were guys making crabmeat, shrimp, and lobster cocktails. The headwaiter made me captain of the parsley. At least six bushels would come in every morning and I had to prepare enough to last the restaurant an entire day. I became very close to the guys while preparing parsley, consequently becoming acquainted with the two white guys who were booking the single-action bets in the restaurant. The place was so big that everyone was betting on the numbers and everyone placed the bets with the waiter.

One day a waiter came into the restaurant with a needle hanging from his arm, obviously high, and talking loudly about taking bets. He caused a major disturbance and was a complete embarrassment. I happened to be standing next to the guys in charge of the numbers game. The waiter was one of their guys. The two white guys turned to me and asked, "Alabama, do you think you can take this single-action for us?"

I replied, "Sure, if you show me what to do."

I confidently promised that by the third day I would be an expert and they would be quite impressed with my work. They agreed to pay me $35 a section. They taught me how to take the single action. The single action was when you bet on odds that were 8 to 1. For instance, a person bets $20 on 3, 6, or 5. If he hits one of them, he would be paid $160 (8 x $20). The person bet on each number individually (single). The winning numbers were announced at 2:20, 3:20, and 4:20. However, each bet had to be taken before the book closed on the hour. (For instance 2:00 for the 2:20 announcement, 3:00 for the 3:20 announcement, and 4:00 for the 4:20 announcement.)

I took all the cooks, waiters, dishwashers, and everyone in the restaurant wanting to bet starting at 1 o'clock. We referred to the two white guys in the restaurant as the mafia boys and they told me that they told the manager of the restaurant, the owner's brother, that I worked for them and not to touch me . . . period. They paid the manager a cut, probably $800 to $1,000 a week, to take the action.

At 2 o'clock I had to stop taking bets. I would come downstairs in the kitchen and give the mafia boys my sheet of paper and all the money. I then went outside to the row of phone booths. I went to the second phone from the right and had to be there no later than 2:15. If there was someone in the booth, I had to buy him or her out or do whatever it took to get the second booth. If I got there early and it was vacant, I would put an out of order sign on the booth. At 2:20 p.m. the phone would ring. I would answer and say, "Blackstone."

A voice would say, "This is Blackstone . . . Annie . . . Annie, Annie."

I had to repeat Annie three times. "A" is the third letter in the word "blackstone." This meant the first number was a three. I had certain signals for certain numbers and there was much anticipation for the numbers. All eyes were on me. I would inform everyone that it was 3 o'clock. I would approach the mafia boys, get the cash, and pay everyone who had the number three. It was like clockwork. This would happen each hour, a total of three times. I thought this was very interesting.

I recall the following year my fraternity brother who attended North Carolina College came to restaurant. He walked in one morning and said, "The Kappa Boat Ride is in two weeks and I'm going to break them today," requesting I play 6-4-8. I agreed to place bets on the six. Word got around in the restaurant that he had the numbers working so everyone bet on the eight. It was the first time in the restaurant when the mafia boys were unable to pay off. They agreed to give everyone an I.O.U. ticket and pay them off the following day. They came in the very next day with a suitcase full of money and paid everyone. They stated that they didn't want anyone to think they were broke. They told me to keep taking bets. This happened again when Muhammad Ali was fighting and everyone bet on Ali. Again the mafia boys had to give I.O.U.s and pay off later.

The mafia boys ran all manner of business through that restaurant, mostly gambling. The mafia boys were salad makers, made all the cocktails, prepared the food for the boss's dogs, and they booked the single-action. They were employees like everyone else. Benny Collins, a black headwaiter, booked the three-number bets. All three numbers had to be correct to win.

After all this, I would rush to prepare for the customers. At 6 o'clock they would come and I was ready. Upstairs would close at 11 o'clock and the night waiters would stay until the restaurant closed at one in the morning. I enjoyed working overtime for a waiter who wanted to leave early. I worked seven days a week and didn't consider taking a day off. I would work from Memorial Day until the Thursday after the Fourth of July—straight through without any days off. On occasion I might take off on a Thursday evening and take a train to Times Square.

HARLEM WAS THE LARGEST congregation of black people in the free world in the sixties. In Harlem, blacks weren't the minority.

I saw Malcolm X preaching on a stepladder. I had never heard the things he had said. He was trashing the white police. He was yelling at the horse police, saying, "We don't need any white police in Harlem!" A black man talking shit to the police? I had never seen anything like that.

I called my mother and told her about the event. This was very unusual to me because I grew up in the South and nothing like this went on there. I loved Harlem from the start. There was energy there, vibrancy. One day I watched Sugar Ray Robinson's car collect dust and sunshine in front of his building. For kicks I went to the Apollo Theater to see several acts like Stevie Wonder, Gladys Knight and the Pips, the Drifters, Redd Foxx, and Flip Wilson. I stayed away from the movies but I remember *Spartacus* was playing.

I made lots of money in New York. I left Lundy's in New York on Labor Day night with more than $7,000 dollars cash. I had seven silk suits, twelve ties, twelve pairs of silk underwear and shorts, two overcoats, and five pairs of nice shoes. I continued to work for Lundy Brothers Restaurant in the summers from 1961 to 1965. New York was good to me. When I think of New York I think of a glorious time and place, full of the grand smells and sights of one of the greatest cities in the world, of numbers rackets, nonstop work, sultry summer nights, and lots and lots of money.

2

A Teacher's Journey

I returned to Alabama State living on one hundred dollars a week and had a dash of the big city clinging to my frame. I wore mohair and sharkskin suits. I had twenty-five ties. The girls blew me out of proportion because I was the only guy on campus with money. And I was sharp as hell. Most of these girls were country girls. "Here he come, y'all," they'd say. "Here he comes." I loved it.

I bought all the girls chicken boxes with some regularity. I'd have those boxes delivered to the dorms. The ladies called me Santa Claus. I wish I had five dollars now for every chicken box I sent to Bibb Graves and Abercrombie halls alone. I'd be rich. I also bought a hundred ties for the Kappas when they serenaded the sweethearts. I paid my tuition for the entire year in September and bought my books. I wore a silk suit every day. When I attended the ball games I would purposely come late to get attention. The ladies would say, "Here he comes."

I fixed shoes, too. I had returned to working at the shoe shop because my father was ill. I was also still working at Pilgrim Life Insurance Company. And I sold jewelry, clothes, everything but dope. I saw what dope did to those cats in Harlem. It caused so much pain and suffering. I had no time for drugs. To me, they only equaled hardship.

One night I made my usual appearance at a ball game and shortly after I sat, two guys came in behind me dragging mink coats and took all my thunder. I was so upset I didn't know what to do. I worked in New York for five years for my style, clothes, and money.

In May 1963, I was expelled from Bama State for keeping my soon-to-be-wife, Mary Lou, out of the dormitory past the stipulated hours. There's more story here, but I'm going to move on.

Everyone decided not to attend the Alabama State College Dance. Dr. Hardy noticed this and decided to have all the young ladies report back to the dorm. Mary Lou and I were out on Ripley Street at a restaurant and her roommate called me and informed us that Mary Lou was reported missing. My two friends were security guards and I asked them to open the left side door to Bibb Graves so that it would be as if she had gone to buy a Coke and some cookies. We tried this and the door was locked. Consequently, I took Mary Lou to my house. Later I had to attend court and was expelled for keeping her out of the dormitory four days before final exams. Some teachers were upset and a few of them allowed me to make up work. Others did not. Mary Lou and I even went to Prattville and got married in an attempt to cover up the incident.

I LEFT FOR New York the very next day. I knew that I really had to work after being expelled. The long, lonely train ride was bittersweet. I was happy to return to the big city, but unsure of what I was going to do for the future.

I returned to Lundy's and continued to wait tables. The headwaiter was glad to see me. Waiters were a very charismatic group. The day waiters wore the old-folk comfort shoes that lace up. They would come out of the kitchen upstairs, kicking the door open with the tray in their hand. They were graceful like ballet dancers. Kids would run by and they would stomp the floor with their leather soles and it would sound like a firecracker.

"Get out of the way!" they would yell, balancing the trays of food and drink with elegant precision. Waiters only cared about themselves and other waiters; no one else existed, save the customer, who only mattered for the tips. A hierarchy existed within the tight-knit group of waiters. There were two older waiters who moved very slowly. They would maneuver about while softly chanting, "Let the good times roll . . . let the good times roll." The young waiters had a lot of respect for the older waiters; they had survived the hustle for a long time.

The cooks also loved me. One of the guys cooking lobster had seen my picture in the *New York Times* helping the ladies onto the National Guard truck. They loved to hear about Dr. King and the bombing of his house.

They were spellbound by the stories I would tell about Dr. King and the South.

I continued to take care of business and was promoted to captain of the Arch Room. The Arch Room needed thirty waiters, all of whom were college students. I was in charge of all the students. Of course, I would put the Kappas on the best station. The Omegas would get upset and make comments about my selections. I just shrugged. No one ever said life was fair.

I enjoyed everyone the entire time I worked at Lundy's.

I GOT BACK INTO school and would go to school during the fall and spring and work at Lundy's in the summer. In 1966, I decided to stay in Montgomery and operate the shoe store. My father was sick in 1962–63. He died in 1964. In 1966 I took over the business. I had a shoe repairer and two shoe shine boys working for me. When my father was alive, he ran the second largest shoe shop in Montgomery.

In the 1960s a black person had to get a white person to "speak" for them in order to get a bank loan or obtain anything of value. The lady that spoke for my father was Mrs. Walker, who taught at Lanier High School. When I graduated college, my mother called Mrs. Walker and asked her to recommend to the superintendent that I be hired to teach. She promised my mother that she would, but her efforts didn't get me a teaching job at that time. I continued to operate the shoe store, run a dice and poker game, and sell cigarettes and beer. In the old days there was only one store in Montgomery open after midnight, and that was the package store on Decatur Street. It was a seller's market.

There were nights when we would be gambling into the early morning and a guy would want a cigarette. My thoughts were that this guy could afford a twenty-dollar pack of cigarettes because of all the money he had won. One guy that stuck in my mind was a white male whose father owned a restaurant across from Gunter Air Force Base. They had the best Italian food in town. He became acquainted with us because one of the waiters who worked for his father's restaurant gambled with us. We always kept a white guy with us when we were gambling. We called him Big Randal. Big Randal was always around. He was heavy-set, sandy-haired, and in his early to mid-twenties. This guy was a true con man. The last I heard of him was that he had pulled a con on some Mormons in Utah, consequently having his photo placed on America's Most Wanted.

After doing a con he would return to Montgomery to my shoe shop. He dropped one-dollar bills from the front door all the way back to the shine stand. As the black kids came in he would say, "Go tell your friends that you've got a stupid white man in here giving away dollar bills."

The young kids would come in and collect the dollar bills, which he thought was good luck. He also loved black females. He said that he loved to talk on the phone to the black women while he took a bath. Big Randal was a strange man. Despite his proclivities, Big Randal was a good guy, and in his own way, honest.

THE GAME WAS REGULAR. We played every night before I owned the club and after I started running my club I played every night the club wasn't open. My brother, Kenneth, ran the poker game when I wasn't there. I had to be at the club. My brother started the game in high school. After eleven, he took over the game, because I had to get ready to teach school the next day.

We were all friends. We cut a dollar out of the hand each night. That money went to furnishing the colas, the beer, the cookies—things to keep the players happy. Every time a new hand was dealt, the houseman would reach in and take a dollar out the pot. The dealer called his own games. Low-Red Even; Texas Hold'em; Seven-Card Stud. I liked Low-Red Even. I deal three cards to everyone. The smallest red, even card was wild. If I dealt a red four, a five of spades, and an ace of hearts, you have three aces. Your lowest card was wild. Your lowest red even was wild. You're trying to get another red four or another match of your lowest card. The more wild cards you got, the better hand you got.

The game was a great thing. But not everyone could play. You had to have a little money; you had to have a little class. We gambled with friends. The only time you gamble with someone you don't know or like is when you go to a casino.

One time a guy I had banned from the game brought the police in an effort to force me to let him play. "Here they are, boss," he stated as he pointed at me.

I explained to the police that the guy was out of control and used too much profanity and that we were all schoolteachers trying to have a good time.

The guy interjected, "Oh, that S.O.B. will let anybody play!"

I sarcastically added, "Do you see what I mean, officer?"

The officer said for us to carry on and took the foul-mouthed guy away. It was funny.

When I married Lucy, my mother called Mrs. Walker again and told her that I had married a young lady from Birmingham, who needed a job. Mrs. Walker stated that she was attending a party that night and would see what she could do. She also asked what I was doing. My mother told her that I never did get a teaching job. Mrs. Walker was shocked. She told my mother that she would see Mr. Garrett, the superintendent, that night and would call her in the morning because he had promised that he would hire me. The following morning she called my mother and told her that I would be hired to teach at Houston Hill Junior High, and that Lucy would be hired to teach at Fews Elementary.

That Monday I was in the shoe shop fixing shoes and the phone rang. It was Mr. Garrett. He said, "Mr. Thomas, I'm looking at your transcript and you made A's in all the mathematics courses you took in college." He went on further to state that there were new Title 1 programs in education and wanted to know if I thought I could teach math to slow learners. I assured him that I could. He said he wanted to put me at Houston Hill because I had minored in industrial arts and Mr. Shores, the industrial arts teacher at Houston Hill, had had a heart attack. "In the event that something happens, you would be ready to assume the role of the industrial arts department," he explained. This sounded like a winner to me. He then linked me with Mr. Edward Stevens who happened to be a member of my church and was over the school textbook committee. Mr. Stevens gave me about forty math textbooks that Montgomery was going to choose as the primary book. I studied each of these books and took ideas from each author on methods to teach fractions, percents, decimals and so forth. These books were based on the modern way of teaching mathematics. I then created a program of my own. I took the slow learners from Tulane Court, Trenholm Court, and North Montgomery and introduced a new way of teaching mathematics.

First, I started with the properties of operation. I would talk about addition being a binary operation. You can only add two numbers at a time. It is also commutative which allows you to change the order and still get the same sum. I would also teach the associative property where the grouping of the adding resulted in the same sum. I taught the properties of multiplication and the distributive properties of multiplication which stated that multiplication is distributive over addition and also that multiplication was a binary operation; you can only multiply two at a time. The students were also taught that the number one was the identity element of multiplication. Any number multiplied by the number one will result in the same number. We also discussed the properties of subtraction and division. I also implemented flash cards for a warm-up drill I did every day in class. On the cards I would write numbers in bold letters like 8, 12, 24, 32, 48, 96 and so on. The properties of operation-additions binary operation, commutative, $3 + 4 = 4 + 3$; box + triangle = triangle + box; funny looking thing + 5 = 5 + funny looking thing associative properties, multiplication, distributive, etc. I taught all this and more. This was in 1966.

I started my classes with warm-up drills, where every child in my class had to be able to factor every composite number less than 100 in their head. When the bell rang I had a bonus problem on the board. The lights would go off, the overhead projector on. Then we'd work with flash cards, 36, 48, 72—even the slower kids had to interject. Every student is going to talk to me at least three times a day and participate in class. Therefore, when it comes to my kids taking standardized tests, there was no hesitation because they understood the properties and executed them efficiently and effectively. I understood that you have to teach a child fractions first, decimals second, and percents third—in that order—as one leads to the other. I noticed the supervisor in the back of the classroom watching in amazement as the class went on. They couldn't believe the progress and participation these "slow learners" were displaying.

The supervisors eventually asked me to give a demonstration of my modern way of teaching mathematics to every teacher in Montgomery for the seventh and eighth grade. These teachers were invited to Houston Hill Junior High to observe my method of teaching. I was indeed ready for the opportunity. I contacted Dr. Robinson and asked him to attend to witness me at my finest hour. He attended, smiling. Beforehand, I told Mrs. Thelma Morris that I was "going to teach these white people that black people know how to teach."

The day finally arrived and all seventh and eighth grade teachers, supervisors, and the superintendent gathered. I glanced in the back and saw Dr. Robinson sitting attentively. I completed my demonstration successfully. Shortly after it was over, the teachers and administrators had a brief session to mingle.

THE PRINCIPAL OF BALDWIN Junior High School, a white school, approached me and said, "Every time I leave these demonstrations I have a feeling that the presentations were planned or rehearsed. However, it is obvious that you planned but I'll be darned if it was rehearsed." He continued to praise me on how effectively the students fell in line with each and every concept put before them. He was very amazed. The administrators then asked me to go to the library. I proceeded there and Dr. Robinson accompanied and chatted with me along the way.

Mrs. Maude Williams came over to the library. Her husband was principal at Georgia Washington school in Mt. Meigs. She told me that the administrators were discussing where they were going to place me next year. Mrs. Williams went on to say that I was going to be the first black teacher to teach at a white junior high school in Montgomery. She told me that the Cloverdale and Goodwyn principals were considering me but she believed that the Cloverdale principal was extremely interested. Besides, Cloverdale had more muscle to recruit and the rich white kids attended Cloverdale.

It was soon declared and I transferred to Cloverdale Junior High School. Now, both Houston Hill and Cloverdale were fine schools. Both had topnotch faculties. Both schools had top black kids. Cloverdale was an elite white school; Houston Hill, before integration, was one of the top black schools. Houston Hill was warmer in the winter. I liked Cloverdale because it was a bit old and ragged; a strong sense of history loomed there.

I brought the modern method there as well as entertained the students along the way. They appeared to be spellbound and captivated with my approach. There were girls of very wealthy and respected parents who ran the city of Montgomery. They entered my classroom with little or no interest in mathematics and before long, they were participating in class and excelling. The president of the Board of Education in Montgomery, Mr. Fred Bear, was also president of Bear Lumber Company. He had built a majority of the dormitories on Alabama State's campus. He called me one evening and told me that he had a grandson in my second period math class and he was having trouble. He continued to say that he understood that it wasn't my fault because he heard that I was the "damn best." He asked me if I would come out on Sundays and tutor his grandson. I responded by saying, "Sir, I don't know if the board will allow me to do that."

Mr. Bear replied, "I am the board. I got your number from the board."

I immediately asked, "Sir, will this Sunday be too soon?"

I worked with his grandson, Bobby Bear, every Sunday for a month and a half. Bobby was soon back on track and doing very well in class. I didn't accept any money from Mr. Bear. I told him that I was doing it as a favor. He thanked me and we went our separate ways. I wasn't in need of any money because I taught school and also ran my gambling game at the shoe shop. Furthermore, I wouldn't have any trouble with the police during my gambling game. If I told Fred Bear that I was having trouble with the police during my gambling game he would certainly be able to fix it. This was how Montgomery operated; prestigious friends trumped the law every time.

As school approached the Christmas holiday break, Mr. Fred Bear pulled up at the shoe shop in a station wagon with twenty Virginia smoked hams. My mother was there taking in shoes to be repaired. He wanted to show his appreciation for my helping his grandson.

After about three years, all the teachers who had integrated the Montgomery public school system, except me, were given promotions to principal, assistant principal, counselor, or another role. I brought this to my supervisor's attention and he stated that he thought I was happy as a teacher. I indicated to him that I loved to teach but I didn't like to maintain records. My lifestyle then—with the shoe shop, poker game, and teaching—was quite busy. Therefore I requested to serve as a liaison between the staff and parents like my fraternity brother did at Capitol Heights school. I stated that I would make everything run smoothly. My supervisor said he would make the transition in January. We mutually agreed.

Bob Gaddis, president of Central Bank on Dexter Avenue, walked in my room early one morning. He said, "Mr. Thomas, I understand that you are trying to leave us. You taught Amy, my oldest daughter, and Meg is in your room now. Do you understand that if you left us, supper wouldn't be the same at my house?" He reminded me that he was the president of the board of trustees at Cloverdale and they had made up their minds that I was not leaving. "I'm sure that's all right with you, isn't it?" he asked in a soft tone.

"Sure, sir, I'm happy," I replied.

As he was walking out the door of my classroom he turned and asked, "Thomas, how's your poker game?" I felt as if he was telling me that if I wanted to keep my poker game I had to keep teaching.

I stayed at Cloverdale and taught until I retired. I taught Artur Davis along with the children of notable families like the Aronovs, Hills, Joe Reed, John Knight, Earl Pippen, Bill Hitchcock, Judge Perry Hooper, Bill Richardson, and Gene Easterling.

I ENJOYED TEACHING EACH and every child, even the difficult ones. And I always stressed the importance of not using or selling drugs. I didn't even want them to smoke cigarettes. I told them that drugs and cigarettes made them ugly and they needed to stay away from them to maintain their beauty. I also stated that the surgeon general stated on each pack of cigarettes that it was hazardous to your health. I followed by saying that this was a nice way of saying that cigarettes would kill you. I went on to say how there were media ploys and motives to addict Americans to cigarettes. I wanted them to know that it was up to them to make a good choice.

Drugs are a very serious thing. When I was in New York at age nineteen, I saw firsthand what cocaine did to all those people in Harlem. I hadn't spoken to my brother Buck in twenty years because I caught him with a roach clip in my ashtray and called the police on him. Any life is preferable to the drug addict's slide into oblivion. Drugs wreck families and ruin lives. I didn't want any part of it and didn't want any student of mine not feeling the same way.

"My idea of getting high is the opposite sex in my arms on a slow number, belly to belly and cheek to cheek," I added. Students who I have taught years ago may run into me in the grocery store. They approach me by saying, "What you do to Peter you must do to Paul." I would smile because what they remembered was how I taught them equations. I would entertain them by adding little demonstrations and informalities to make it fun. I would tell the girls, "What you do to Peter you must do to Paul. If you kiss Peter you must kiss Paul. If you give Paul some sugar you've got to give Peter some sugar even though Peter doesn't look as good as Paul."

Then they would go home and tell their parents.

My girls at Cloverdale thought enough of me to nominate me for Man of the Year against a slew of well-known Montgomery men. Their parents called me when I tried to get out of it and said, "Mr. Thomas, those other girls who made nominations don't even know their Man of the Year; they just go to church with them, but your girls know you and they really believe that you are their Man of the Year." I didn't think I could win and didn't really want to but they said it would be a big let-down if I didn't attend the ceremony with them. So I went out to the Governor's House Ballroom. I sat at the table with thirty white girls and represented this chapter for Man of the Year. I think it took them about a minute to read my accomplishments in life and about fifteen minutes to read Winton Blount's, a former postmaster general under the Nixon administration. He reorganized the postal service and his company, Blount Industries, built material for the space ship. C. T. Fitzpatrick owned the Governor's House and the Diplomat Motel.

Running against people like that, I obviously lost. But I like to think it was close between me and Winton Blount, the most famous man from Montgomery.

I knew a lot of people in Montgomery, including one of the nicest guys I ever met, Federal Judge Frank Johnson, Jr., in the Middle District of Alabama. Judge Johnson was involved in most of the major civil rights cases in Alabama and he always sided with the good guys. But he also went out of his way to explain the process to black people. I once made a bond for a guy and Johnson called me into his chambers. He explained politely what would happen if the guy fled and how the bond system worked.

I considered him a friend. I spent some time around him. I even fixed his back brace one Sunday morning. One of the things about Judge Johnson was that he was from the hill country of Winston County in north Alabama. They didn't have many slaves up there and a lot of the white people were Lincoln Republicans. Judge Johnson had a different approach and wasn't quick to make a generalization of all blacks.

THE CLOVERDALE GIRLS LIKED me because I taught them how to compete with the boys in mathematics. I'd go to football games and twelve white cheerleaders would run over and hug me. This wasn't popular with the older generation. So this poor white cop puts a rumor out that I was fooling with white students. This was out there, even though I was innocent. Soon after the rumor, Judge Johnson sent me a note saying, be careful. He said he was so proud of me, showing everyone how a black man can teach. He said, just be careful. He said he couldn't bus the white kids to the black school. The black kids would do better by being bused to the white school. He said this was the best he could do. I wish we had more judges like him.

Principal Ed Richardson asked all the teachers to eat with the kids to establish rapport and teach table manners. I ate with my students just as he asked us to. The students liked lunch time. I continued to teach as we ate, although in an informal manner. I remember the math department head at Cloverdale coming to my room and she said, "Mr. Thomas, they are transferring students to you in the middle of the year. What do you think about that?"

Midway through the semester, a number of students asked to transfer into my math class. I said I didn't question the ones they sent in September. I didn't question the office. I taught who they sent. They knew I could teach thirty better than I could forty but evidently they thought I could handle it, so I handled it. I didn't question, I just taught and did the best I possibly could.

There was a young lady named Vickie who worked at my club as a bartender. She was attending Auburn University at Montgomery. She was having difficulty understanding percents in a math class and had a test the next night. The waitress I'd taught at Cloverdale worked at my club and told her that I was the best at teaching mathematics. She said, "He's going to yell at you, curse you out, and call you stupid, but after four hours you will be the best in the class. If you listen to that fool, you'll be the best." She came up to the club that night and I taught her percents. She appeared to understand and thanked me. She then goes to AUM, takes a fifty-problem test, and gets them all correct with the exception of one. A white female in her class has the same result. Ironically, they missed the same problem. The teacher noticed that both individuals sat on opposite sides of the classroom and couldn't have possibly cheated. She then asked Vickie who tutored her with percents. Vickie stated, "My boss at Top Flight, Mr. Thomas."

The white female smiled and said, "He taught me at Cloverdale."

I thought this was pretty amazing. And, statistically speaking, close to miraculous.

I taught mathematics by associating it with things in life. I would use the percents discussion to talk about cocaine. I would ask, "Why would you buy cocaine from someone not knowing what percentage of it was cocaine? Furthermore, why would you buy drugs to put in your body from some fool who doesn't have a medical degree? You can't be that stupid and call yourself a student of mine," I added. I told them that this is why you find the opposite sex, get belly-to-belly and check-to-check and dance to a slow number, while leaving the cocaine alone. I diligently stressed the importance of school and staying away from drugs.

An irony about all this is that the guy who came to my house on February 17, 1994, in charge of the task force to arrest me for the conspiracy to distribute cocaine in the Middle District of Alabama, was Bert Bodiford, one of the students I had taught all this to at Cloverdale. He was one of a few of my white male students who went into law enforcement.

The majority of the white male students I taught became doctors and lawyers. Bodiford was a deputy sheriff on loan to the task force. The task force consisted of men from the local police department, sheriff's department, DEA, FBI, ABI, and ABC Board. They formed the task force, working together on drug cases. This is how they operate. But I'm getting ahead of the story.

Lewis Franklin, prosecutor of the Middle District of Alabama, and Judge Myron Thompson of the Middle District of Alabama—people risked their lives and some were killed so the two of you could have a job in the federal building. You owe Dr. King and Rosa Parks a commitment to make things right in the federal building named after Frank Johnson, Jr., the man who helped you get a job in that building in the first place. When I went to Cloverdale School, they didn't need a good math teacher; they needed a good black math teacher who would be fair to all students, rich, poor, black, white, Iranian and Vietnamese. I always will believe that Marshall Simmons, DEA head, knew I shouldn't have been indicted. He knew I wasn't involved with drugs in any way. By him lying to the grand jury, like many white men of power, he let those few corrupt white men do what they want to do to minorities. They conveniently forget they are in law enforcement.

3

THE TOP FLIGHT

In December 1979, I opened the Top Flight night club at 954 Highland Avenue in Montgomery. I bought the building from Mr. Isaac Cohen. My black godfather, Frank Armstead, had operated Club Delisa here in the sixties. He made the bar revolve like a merry-go-round. And he had a dance floor that rose up with the touch of a button. His daughter worked the door for him and she was a classmate of mine. So even though I was only nineteen, she would let me into the club. Now, the Commodores came in around '67. At that time, they were just some Tuskegee guys who played some music. With a black disc jockey, they formed the Metric East Club and occupied the building. Then they lost interest and left. The vacant building then deteriorated for ten years. In 1978, Frank Armstead came into my shoe shop and asked me to buy the building. The nearby St. Margaret's Hospital was expanding in this direction and he said for $3,000 down and $210 a month for fifteen years, the building would be mine. He said, we'll open it up Thanksgiving for a night club. So, I bought the building and went to work. My industrial arts background came in handy. I worked on the building from July 1978 to Thanksgiving Eve 1979, when the Health Department came out and approved me. I got a whiskey license and hired some people. I opened December 7, 1979. She was a hit from the beginning. We packed this place in.

I had made it beautiful. All those months of hard work, where I shined and sanded and stained and nailed and everything else, paid off. We had spotless bathrooms. We had all-new chairs, tables, speakers, and lights. The dance floor still moved up at the hit of a button. The disco ball spun around. We had disco music blaring and people came to dance and drink and be merry. Top Flight was the best club in Montgomery, if I do say so myself.

I didn't have a parking lot at first. I saved up enough money to buy all the property across the street, however. We tore down the houses and buildings and paved over the wreckage and that problem was solved. I ran Top Flight through the eighties. She did quite well. And every time I made some money, I put it back into the building. I had big screen televisions when Tyson was kicking it in the mid-1980s. Everything was first class.

I loved working at the club, but then again I love to work. I did everything myself, everything. During the days I was teaching at Cloverdale, helping those white and black kids learn math. I finished around 3 and went directly to Top Flight. I ordered my beer or my whiskey, my skins, potato chips—something to eat. Then I got to work. I made the necessary repairs. I waxed and sprayed and cleaned and dusted and double-checked. And then I'd open that night. Thursday night was college night. I would work all night and get home at 5:30 A.M. I'd shave, shower, powder my nose, and then report to work at Cloverdale. Sometimes I would put up flyers, so I wouldn't even get home until 6:15.

I believe you rest when you die. And when I die, I'll rest a long, long time. While I'm here, I'm ready to work. No one ever said, "You look sleepy, Richard," or "You need to get more rest." I like to work. I thrive on it. The club and the teaching and the shoe shop and the poker game and my family: this was my life. And I had time, stamina, and energy enough for it all. I was a worker; still am, I suppose. I did everything that was necessary. Cleaning the stools, emptying ashtrays, bartending. I trained the new employees—anything that was needed. I even played the happy hour music on Fridays. Sometimes a kid from Alabama State would come up and earn some deejay experience.

For years, we had the biggest happy hour in town. I started the Friday evening happy hour. You weren't anybody in Montgomery if you weren't at Top Flight's Happy Hour. All the black Air Force guys in the War College came, as did all the Saudi Arabia guys in their war college. The Saudi guys are now in charge of the Saudi Arabian air force. They became friends of mine through the club. In '98, they offered me a flight to Zurich, where they were going to pick me up on one of their planes. I said, no way. You couldn't pay me to leave this country. If something happened, I'd never get back. Not many people know this, but during the Iran hostage affair, the Iranians had a black guy with them. And they sent him back with the women and children. Because they knew America wouldn't pay a quarter to get a black hostage released. So it goes.

MY CUSTOMER BASE WAS huge and diverse. I had U.S. marshals, judges, police. For a while it was a who's who of Montgomery privilege: Alfred Seawright, Greg Calhoun, Alvin Holmes, James Hall, Judge Charles Price. They all hung out in here on Friday evenings. They would leave around 9:30 when the volume turned up on the music and the young people took over. They wouldn't leave until 1:30. Then we'd have another crowd at 2 o'clock, the third shift at National Industries, owned by June Collier.

I had great staff, including Clinton Brown, the HNIC at the Alabama Supreme Court. He kept the peace in Top Flight.

One day Sinbad, the comedian, came through Montgomery. He was famous, one of the most famous. So he comes to the club and Brown asks for eight dollars, the cover charge for that night.

"I'm Sinbad," he said.

And Brown said, "Buddy, I don't know you from Jack the Playboy. Eight dollars." So Sinbad paid, and a friend told me that the next night, he incorporated it into his act.

We had the best music in the Deep South. The best R&B bands, before this hard rap stuff took over, toured through Top Flight. We had music and comedians. We had the Manhattans, Bobby Blue Bland, and Roger and Zapp, a funky band that put on the best show I've ever seen here. Roger Troutman was his name, I think. He played with two pipes in the side of his mouth. He put on a show. I mean a show.

We had Millie Jackson perform, as well as LaWanda Page (Aunt Esther from Sanford and Son). They were two of the first black female comedians to talk about men. I remember Aunt Esther came here and she sat on the stage with a dress slit up all the way to her waist. And she made up lies about me all night long. She sang suggestive songs and mocked the shortcomings of men everywhere and she was a hit. Outkast performed here, before they were sued by Rosa Parks. H Town performed here, during the time when they had their hit song, "Knockin' the Boots." I had every hot group in Atlanta perform here. Everybody played Top Flight.

Then the music shifted to hard rap music. Although I kind of like Tupac and a few of Biggie Smalls's songs, the rap generally wasn't as good; it lacked soul. And it was violent. I would tell people: the Manhattans have toured for thirty years, and they've never shot anyone or been shot at.

Yes, Frank Armstead had been right. Top Flight was a great investment. It made me a lot of money and I enjoyed the work. It put me at the center of things. We had a few fights here and there but my people took care of things and it was a great club and everyone liked it.

THE TROUBLE STARTED IN January 1994. At some point in the late 1980s, the game had changed. There were more guns. The drugs were harder. And the street gangs that used to fist fight over a corner were now gunning each other down for the same twenty feet of concrete.

In '94, major incidents went down. A kid named Nesbitt came up Jackson and High streets and killed two boys in a gunfight, one of them his friend. He had been at a night club on Atlanta Highway, nowhere near Top Flight. But after an altercation at the first place, he ended up downtown. He spotted the boy he'd had his problems with at a shrimp restaurant near my club.

My security guard heard the first gunshot. He ran over to the corner of Jackson and High and saw Nesbitt shoot the second boy in cold blood. So my security guard fired on him. Nesbitt drove off but he'd been hit. The cops found him over on Atlanta Highway.

It was a big story. And, as usual, the *Montgomery Advertiser* got the details all wrong. They said that the boys involved had been in Top Flight, although one of them had been banned from entry months before. They put the bodies on my doorstep. I confronted the editors and they acknowledged they'd made a mistake. But they didn't print a retraction. This hurt Top Flight's reputation.

The *Advertiser*'s misinformed coverage connected Top Flight to a gang-style shoot-out. This wasn't good for business. The paper didn't care about the damage they did me, nor would they care later. They sold their papers and the story was hot. Who cares about the details? This same type of laziness—or dishonesty, lack of ethics, bad reporting, whatever you want to call it—hurt me again and again. The *Montgomery Advertiser* established a pattern with the first lies they told about me. They would continue to hurt me in the years to come.

America's Prison Problem

We incarcerate more people than any other country in the world, including communist China, a totalitarian state which we regularly criticize for its human rights violations.[1] Although we call ourselves the freest country in the world, we have to face a hard fact: either we're imprisoning people for bad reasons, or there's something fundamentally wrong with our society. The American justice system has run amok. It's racist, profit-oriented, and out of control.

This chapter is an interlude, a break from my struggles with Assistant U.S. Attorney Charles Teschner and my problems with the justice system in Alabama. I'm providing this information to try and influence the minds of Americans. This polemic is backed up by facts and the hard reality of my own experiences; I've added endnotes so that people can go learn some more on their own. A second interlude deals with the so-called war on drugs, but for now I want to talk about the American prison system.

I started thinking about this book by running over the way I was treated by the law. Now in my life, I've been the victim of racial prejudice. Most people nowadays think of racial prejudice as dirty looks on buses or bad service in restaurants. This kind of stuff still happens and although no black person likes it, we can live with it. After the civil rights movement, I think most white folks just sort of turned their heads, deciding that black people had been given enough help. And a lot of middle-class black folks accepted that we now had the right to vote, we could date who we wanted (for the most part), and we weren't being lynched every other day—let's leave it alone.

What I'm saying is, most people thought that racial prejudice was bad, but we can live with it. And we do, every day.

Racial prejudice in the law and legal system, however, is lacerating the black population. And the cuts run deep. From the prejudiced cops who assume guilt when they pull black people over to the prejudiced prosecutors who assume guilt and push for maximum sentencing to the prejudiced judges who throw the book at black youths they've assumed are irredeemable, the legal system in this country hates black people. Our prisons are racist and examples of a double standard in our legal system are not hard to find. This hurts the cause of justice and creates angry black youths who have no faith in their country or in justice.

So let's take a look at the prison system in the United States. Let's take a look at the facts.

ONE OUT OF THREE black men between the ages of twenty and twenty-nine is in the criminal justice system in one way or another.[2] This is a staggering number, even to a math teacher like me. Thirteen percent of monthly drug users are black. But blacks are being incarcerated at a rate of ten to one over whites. They are twice as likely to receive prison time and the sentence will be 20 percent longer.[3]

Look at the numbers. Numbers, as I mentioned before, don't lie. From 1986 to 1991, the number of African American males incarcerated on drug charges increased by 429 percent. Some 65 percent of our nation's prisoners never finished high school; 33 percent were unemployed at the time of their arrest; and 32 percent had jobs but were earning less than $5,000 a year.[4] Prisons are a repository of our country's poor.

Blacks are 7.66 times as likely to be incarcerated than whites. Crack users are 64 percent white, only 26 percent black. Yet, 91 percent of the inmates imprisoned for crack sales were black. Sentencing guidelines for crack cocaine impose penalties 100 percent greater than for the powdered form, despite the drugs being almost identical. Cocaine powder is a rich man's drug; crack is a drug of the street.[5]

I'll translate the above statistics for you: if you're poor and black and you run afoul of the drug laws, you don't have a prayer.

In my own experiences, the justice system went out of its way not to prosecute white defendants, but tried to loop in as many black defendants as possible. Evidence pointed towards the Hill brothers, for instance, but in my opinion the evidence was ignored because they're rich and white.

PRISONS ARE ALSO BIG business.

Law enforcement costs a lot of money, and therefore it makes someone a lot of profit. Accounting for guards, security, weapons, training, as well as the beds, prison bars, flooring, uniforms, cereal, toilet paper and so on, these contracts to the prisons are very lucrative.[6] The whole apparatus makes huge profits. Prison is a society—there are beds, towels, linens, snacks, telephone calls, and so on. These services are provided by private companies that bid on the contracts. The contracts are lucrative precisely because they have such a captive audience. Prisoners do not have the option to buy a different brand of crackers or use another telephone service; there is no free market in prison. The result is a system that guarantees maximum profits for itself—through kickbacks to the prisons—without any regulation. The company that offers the highest cost towards to the prisoner often wins the bid; the exact opposite of free-market philosophy.[7]

Prisoners also need healthcare, doctors, dentists, medications, and so on. But the state of healthcare in most prisons is dismal. Author Joel Dyer, in his book, *The Perpetual Prison Machine*, talks about this very thing: "The less healthcare these corporations actually provide to the prisoner, the more money they get to keep for themselves."[8]

It makes sense. Prisoners in the U.S. are viewed by the vast majority of citizens as evil men deserving of terrible conditions. A similar situation exists with the popular conception of drugs. All prisoners are seen in the same light. Never mind that a huge chunk of the prison population is composed of nonviolent offenders, some of whom didn't even know they were breaking the law. In the public mind, they are all bad. Just as all drugs—uppers, downers, amphetamines, hallucinogens, and the rest—are all bad.

I'm not a prisoner and I don't now nor have I ever used drugs. But the system as it exists is spiraling out of control.

More prisons equal more jobs and more money for someone.

This is a hard thing to consider but it's true. Building new prisons is a smart economic move. Construction and maintenance of prisons has rein-vigorated fledgling economies in rural areas. People now want prisons to be built in their towns.[9] The contractors need workers, supplies, places to stay, places to eat. The new prisons need guards, drivers, and other support people. Many towns see new prisons as economic development.

The current system of high incarceration rates and ever-increasing facilities to deal with the overcrowding of today's prisons did not happen in a vacuum. Joel Dyer, again, points out three reasons why prisons are important gateways to power:

1. The accelerating consolidation of the media industry
2. The rise in influence of political consultants
3. The emergence of an organized prison-industrial complex that is perhaps best described as a collection of interests whose financial well-being rises and falls with the size of the prison population.[10]

All prisons are partly privatized. Tax dollars are diverted from other programs to pay for the construction of new prisons—all without voter ap-proval.[11] The recent trend is towards outsourcing prison operations to private contractors. Major corporations have their fingers in the prison honeypot: Disney, Microsoft, American Express, and AT&T, to name a few.[12] Not all of the corporations involved are American, and many own prisons all over the world. And they—with lobbyists and campaign contributions—help mold public policy. Foreign companies dictate to some degree internal legal policies.[13]

A handful of transnational monopolies (roughly nine) owning everything is not free market capitalism.[14]

These corporations spend funds to elect or influence politicians who will continue to put people in prison, therefore continuing profits. Everyone benefits, save the taxpayers, the prisoners, and the overall moral fabric of our country.[15] In return, media companies receive public tax dollars to create anti-drug advertisements, thus reinforcing the perception of rampant drug use. It's a vicious circle of business, profits, and money.[16]

It's politically expedient to be tough on crime.

Crime will never completely go away. It's been a reality of human existence since the first people banded together around a fire to form a tribe. The "War on Crime" is a misnomer.[17] The whole attitude is based on a platitude. No one really believes that the various forms of lawbreaking that constitute "crime" will ever disappear. But politicians beat the "crime" issue to bolster their approval ratings. It's a very effective way to be voted into office. And to stay there.[18] The surest way not to get elected is to propose some measure of clemency towards convicted felons.

Money wins elections. This is a cold, hard fact of the American political system. Money is raised through donations, often from individuals who are executives of big corporations. Many donors give money to candidates they believe can win. This "winnability" factor is often controlled through a media blitz overseen by the millionaire political consultants that have risen to such power in the second half of the twentieth century. The interchangeable consultants utilize basic political formulas for their candidates. Be positive about jobs. Be of the people in your tastes. And always be tough on crime. This pleases the large corporations just fine. Remember, many of them profit from the prison industry.[19]

Dyer argues that only tough-on-crime candidates receive donor funds, as only tough-on-crime candidates can win. The result is a political natural selection, a weeding out of candidates that don't kowtow to this particular point of view. Both political parties claim to be tough on crime. This adds to the overall self-perpetuating problem of the perception of crime, and to "solutions" based on these fabricated concepts. Politicians talk tough on crime because it's what they think the voters want to hear. Voters respond to these hard-line speeches. It's a never-ending circle, a mobius strip. As the voters respond, the consultants latch onto the very message that is being responded to. The candidate's numbers rise. And the donations from corporation bosses keep coming in.[20]

CRIME IS NOT OUR nation's biggest problem. Drugs are not our nation's biggest problem. Poverty, inequality, crumbling public education (in some areas), the economy—these are the issues, the causes of crime.[21] Everyone knows what causes crime: poverty. Almost anyone is potentially a thief if he or she is hungry. The biggest deterrent to crime: jobs. When the economy is humming, crime rates decrease. When American companies outsource labor to other countries on a large scale, they are contributing to a situation that will result in more criminals.[22] These same companies then reap the benefits from their own amoral actions by profiting from the chaotic situations of despair and hopelessness that they created in the first place.

It's a vicious circle that appears to be self-perpetuating.

Criminals are made, not born. Create the right set of circumstances and anyone—Abe Lincoln, Franklin Roosevelt, even Jesus—will commit petty larceny to survive. (And Jesus was considered a criminal; the most perfect man in history was executed for breaking the law.)

The situation isn't getting better. Each new candidate, presidential or otherwise, talks about getting tougher on crime, to have an ante over his or her opponent. The result is an arms race of criminal sentencing. The problem is, the zero-tolerance, three-strike laws that have become de rigeur are creating more criminals, not fewer. Gut-level assumptions that harder sentences plus more incarcerated equals less crime are utterly false.[23] The lock-them-up-until-they-die approach isn't working.[24] When crime is down, politicians credit the prison system and thus advertise the need for more prisons. When crime is up, politicians talk about the need for more prisons. The answer, then, is always more prisons.

In 1984, parole was abolished in federal prisons. "Life" in jail in England is thirty years. In Sweden, each prisoner has internet access. The problem with removing parole is that the prison apparatus then has no way of rewarding good behavior. We can punish bad behavior, sure, by tacking on extra years to a sentence or remove certain amenities. But these punitive actions are not motivators, just as harsher laws don't actually cut into serious crimes. We have to bring back the early-parole-for-good behavior system.[25] Without the possibility early release for good behavior—the only thing any prisoner really desires—the powers that be can only try and control prison populations with the stick.

Mandatory sentencing is another misstep in the "War on Drugs" and the larger prison culture. Mandatory sentences prevent a judge from doing just that: judging, using his judgment. Mandatory minimum sentences disallow consideration of extenuating circumstances and prior history.[26] These mandatory minimums in federal drug cases, combined with the absence of any parole, have resulted in an explosion in long-term inmates, many incarcerated for nonviolent crimes. Violent felons are often cycled through various jail systems faster than nonviolent drug offenders.[27] This isn't right. If anyone should be in prison, it should be violent offenders.

Steven Donziger in *Atlantic Monthly* makes the same point I did earlier, referring to politicians, when he quotes the current thinking on crime: "If crime is going up, then we need to build more prisons; and if crime is going down, it's because we built more prisons—and building even more prisons will therefore drive crime down more than ever."[28]

Prison brings out the worst in everyone.

The prison setting—with dilapidated concrete buildings, open-air toilets, no privacy, no sanctity of anything, and housing together millions of desperate men with no hope—has resulted in a moral quagmire that has trapped the guards, wardens, politicians, and every single citizen of the U.S. Even innocent people are corrupted by prison. In a process called "prisonization," each new prisoner learns the criminal codes of prison; this is an adaptive function necessary to an individual's survival in prison.[29]

This prison culture of physical and sexual violence, intimidation, harassment, and force results in tarnished, hate-filled people when they are released. Their good parts have been scooped out, replaced with all the vile, sick, sad things of human nature. Inside prisons, innocent people become criminals. Criminals become killers. And all are that much further away from any sort of rehabilitation. Nonviolent criminals, forced into a vicious cycle, become hardened, habituated to criminal life. Their continued survival depends on it.[30]

We have no real data to the rate of sexual assault in prison. But it's high, really, really high. We know that.[31] A 1968 report on prisons in Philadelphia found two thousand sexual assaults in a one-year period. "Virtually every slightly built young man committed to jail by the courts—many of them merely to await trial—is sexually approached within hours of being behind bars. Many young men are overwhelmed and repeatedly 'raped' by gangs of inmate aggressors." In 1996, author James Gilligan in his book, *Violence* . . . , reported that sexual assaults in prison occurred at a rate close to nine million a year.[32]

How many innocent people have to be raped and mauled before things change? Or, perhaps more importantly, how much do convicted felons have to endure before even they are given basic protections?

It isn't a surprise that people who spend years in this environment, guilty or otherwise, come out of prison more likely to commit crimes. You cannot subject a human being to years of physical, mental, and emotional assault, provide no real training, and limit his or her prospects at the end of this period and expect an upright citizen to emerge. Recidivism is a product of failed rehabilitation. Looking at the recidivism numbers, it's obvious that ex-convicts have trouble adapting to non-prison life. Then they commit new crimes, starting the cycle over. This undercuts the whole purpose of prison—to keep the streets as safe as possible.

The media is driven by profits generated by advertising.

When their market share is up, they can charge more per second of advertising. They thus need more viewers. By focusing on fear and disproportionately on crime, television news scares viewers into watching.[33] The data concerning violence in entertainment is staggering, Dyer writes. By the time the average American kid turns eighteen, he or she has witnessed more than 200,000 acts of simulated violence from movies and television.[34] In many ways, we're living in an unparalleled period of peace and prosperity, even taking into account the threat of terrorism. Think about it: crime rates are uniformly down, save for a few trouble spots like poor Baltimore. Our streets are as safe as they have ever been. Yet, doesn't everyone feel an ominous sense of danger? It's manufactured.

In return, media companies receive public tax dollars to create anti-drug advertisements, thus reinforcing the perception of rampant drug use. It's a vicious circle of business, profits, and money.[35]

The statistics concerning crime rates and incarceration are misrepresented for propaganda use. You can see a similar phenomenon in the "missile gap" propaganda used to great effect in the late 1950s.[36]

Government employees in oversight positions often end up working for the industry they were earlier supposed to be regulating. This kind of incestuous revolving-door employment isn't uncommon, but it does not protect the public trust.[37]

Prisons are a huge drain on public resources. It would be cheaper, and there would be less crime, to fund a public works project and put nonviolent felons to work. This isn't a political statement. It's a practical solution. Look at the recidivism rates. The effects of prisonization. The spiraling costs. The unchecked suffering.[38] Prisons are a blight on our countryside, on our resources, on our people.

Politicians seeking office. A population scared by decades of inflated criminal reporting and hyper-violent entertainment content. Vast corporations raking in unheard-of profits. While American citizens, some guilty, some innocent, are bulldozed into a hellish life that guarantees suffering and further destabilizes the republic. Mere rhetoric holds the system in place. And billions of dollars in profits.[39]

Things can be done to improve the situation, some simple, some not. First, prisons should be in the domain of the government. Philosophically, the State (whether it be federal or state government) enforces laws through application of the Constitution. The founding fathers weren't sure how to logically and consistently create a system that guaranteed rights and upheld laws—in the wake of the divine right of the British monarchy. The result was a rigorous outline of our legal rights and responsibilities. This flexible, breathing document, along with the Declaration of Independence, is the cornerstone of our legal system and our democracy. The State is empowered by people, individuals. It acts in our name. "When these laws are girded too tight . . ." Sometimes the State has to make hard decisions, especially at the edges of crime and law.

But by what right do private companies imprison people? Where is it written, or implied, that the State can sell citizens to companies' care? How is this legal? (We know it is immoral.)

We have to puncture the myths concerning crime, the war on drugs, and prisons. Many people who go to prison are innocent!

Criminals are not a cause of destruction in this country; they are an effect of our country's loss of faith in its fundamental ideals.

Second, better job training is required.[40] Prisoners should have to work. They should also have to learn a real trade. Like when an undergraduate has to declare a major in college, prisoners should have to choose certain trades, such as mechanics, carpentry, or more intellectual pursuits such as law, then take classes, and work at it. This would leave many ex-convicts in a much better position when they are released from jail. At the moment, jobs in prisons do not help prisoners with jobs in real life. There is no incentive for initiative. There is no reason to work hard. There is no concept of teamwork. You're given one small, boring, often-inane job to do and you do it, for years.[41] Perhaps even an internship program, where soon-to-be ex-convicts work at a place to learn the ropes, and graduate from prison with a job.

Third, prisoners should be required to earn a GED to get out of jail. Except in certain cases where mental deficiency is an issue, prisoners should, as a preamble to freedom, have a high school diploma. They should be forced to take classes in English, math, and so on. Education is the first step towards empathy. Empathy is the first step towards seeing other people as individuals and not manifestations of yourself. Education is one road to ending narcissism. And it opens financial doors.

Finally, employment restrictions for ex-convicts must be removed. The major reason why people go into jail in the first place, besides our corrupt drug laws which I will deal with later, is the lack of economic possibility. Ex-convicts have earned the right to reenter American society. They should therefore have the right of privacy returned to them. Otherwise, it's more of the same. And we all keep on paying.

Mere rhetoric holds the system in place. And billions of dollars in profits.[42]

4

GUILTY BY ASSOCIATION

A school teacher who owned and operated a night club: that was me. I now had influence with the elite students of Montgomery during the day and pull with the elite adults of Montgomery at night. The popularity of the Top Flight put me in an interesting cross-section of people. I was nice to everyone; everyone was welcome.

The club, where I spent most of my free time, is where I met Curtis Drayton. The first time I noticed Curtis was at my happy hour; he was well-dressed with bright colors. I went in the kitchen one Friday and saw my waitress in the kitchen fixing her hair and putting on more perfume. She said, "Squirrel, that sharp guy out front tipped me twenty last week, and I've got him down for forty tonight when I finish rubbing these big legs on him and he's smelling this perfume when I'm bringing him these drinks."

This made me start noticing this guy. Some way or another, this guy weaved his way into our circle: U.S. Marshal Joe Merriweather, James Harrell, Judge Price, Tokey Cummings, Greg Calhoun, Alfred Seawright, etc. We had a social group called the Gentleman's Club and he got in with us. He was mostly welcomed when he came in the club with the Hill brothers. I knew who the Hill boys were when I taught their older brother at Cloverdale when I integrated it in 1968. I'd been to their home several times and knew who they were. They were the sons of a prominent Montgomery family, old money, powerful in politics. When I saw Curtis with them, I automatically assumed that Curtis was somebody and so did my friends.

I would only beep Curtis for the poker game or tell him if I was going to have a big show at the club. As a business owner, you don't worry about what a customer is doing and it's not your business. All you know is they spend a pretty good bit of money and you want them there for that and to have a good time. This was the extent of my relationship with Curtis—friendly, but not too interested. We played cards together sometimes and that was about it. This is why the uproar on February 16, 1994, was so alarming.

On February 16, 1994, the task force arrested everyone on their list. I wasn't picked up because I was in Atlanta for the day. Unbeknownst to me, the gauntlet had been thrown down. When I returned to Montgomery that evening, I had a few precious hours left. I never expected such a dark chain of events to occur that destroyed my life and everything I had worked so hard for.

The next day at 1 P.M. my doorbell rang. I looked outside through the peephole and saw jackets displaying the FBI, DEA, Montgomery Sheriff's Department, Montgomery Police Department, and the ABC Board. I opened the door; I was calm but curious. One of the officers asked if they could come in. I agreed without hesitation. The moment I let them enter they all rushed in and scattered in all directions. I asked what was going on. A man approached me and said, "Mr. Thomas, we have a warrant to arrest you for the conspiracy to distribute cocaine in the Middle District of Alabama." I told him that he had to be crazy. "I gamble but I don't fool with cocaine, period," I said. "I don't even smoke."

"I'm agent Bodiford," he said. "We have a warrant for your arrest on conspiracy charges to distribute cocaine in the Middle District of Alabama. Do you mind going with us?" He showed me the warrant. I agreed to cooperate fully. I was wearing a pair of shorts and a T-shirt so I asked if they would allow me to put on more clothes. I urged them to follow me while I put on pants and another shirt. As I was heading for the door, I saw Larry Armstead, who was head narcotics officer on the Montgomery police force. I knew Larry Armstead from Top Flight and from college. Armstead was an Omega and came to my club during happy hour most Fridays.

I asked Larry what this was all about. He said he didn't know.

"You know I'm not involved with cocaine," I said.

"I've already told them that, Squirrel," he said.

The U.S. marshals joined our conversation. One of the marshals approached me and said, "Mr. Thomas, we want to see your yearbooks so we can see what Bert looked like in the eighth grade." It was then I realized Bert was my former student, and he was one of the officers in charge. It became apparent to me that Bert Bodiford had a previous conversation with the marshals about me teaching him in the eighth grade. I had taught Bert all about mathematics and lectured his entire class about the evils of drug use. I relaxed. Surely Bert knew I didn't fool with cocaine or any other narcotics. I knew there was nothing to this. I had absolutely no dealings with cocaine; one of the major officers was a former student; this would pass before sundown.

Once again I asked Larry Armstead, "Will you tell these people I don't fool with any drugs?"

Larry repeated that he had told them.

After hearing this, my former student, Bodiford said, "Mr. Thomas, since you claim you don't fool with cocaine you shouldn't mind us searching your home or club for cocaine."

"Of course not," I replied. I then told Larry Armstead not to let anyone plant any drugs in my home. If they found anything remotely suspicious, I'd go to prison.

"If they find a cigarette butt in my home, I'll do two years," I said.

"I know that, I've already told them," Larry assured.

"Then we can start searching?" Bodiford asked.

"Of course," I said.

They started the search and didn't find any drugs or drug paraphernalia. They then entered my walk-in closet and found nothing. A lot of agents were milling around at this point. I learned later that this was a special task force, which is why they had so many different types of law enforcement people. I didn't even recognize some of the departments. Then Bodiford's voice called me into my walk-in closet. I followed him in there and we stood in front of my safe.

"Mr. Thomas, open your safe," Bodiford said.

"My life savings are in this safe. There is no cocaine in there," I said.

"Well, then open it," Bodiford replied.

I stared at the safe and felt immense pressure. I knew Bodiford, not well but he had been a former student, and I still, at this point, sort of believed in the rightness of law enforcement, in justice. See, I'm a black man with a strange way of living. All I did was work. I'm black, but I'm no nigger. I worked. I worked my whole life and didn't spend any of my money. Those agents should have thought of me as a Black Jew. I live like a Jewish man. I do everything with saving money on my mind. But they didn't. They saw a nigger in the South with a safe in his closet and they assumed the worst. So I bent down and made the biggest mistake of my life. I opened the safe. And Bodiford saw all that money, and he grabbed it. He stuffed my life's savings into evidence bags without giving me a receipt for any of it. I had money in there I had made more than thirty years ago.

They found $4,500 I made in New York in 1961 that I swore I would never depart from. They found another $4,500 stacked neatly that I made by selling my shoe repair equipment to a guy in Atlanta. Another $48,000 was found where I hit the Florida Fantasy Five on September 26, 1990. The rest of the money I made was shoved into the safe. I'd been gambling for thirty something years and every day I left the house I would have $150. All the money I made over $150 would go into the safe. I worked all the time and didn't have time to count money. I drove a 1969 Grand Prix for thirty-two years. I had Christmas presents inside the trunk of my car, some of which I placed in the safe were over fifteen years old. I never made time to open presents or count money. My primary focus was on my business. It was a huge wad of cash.

They also took Sylvester Harvey's diamond ring and Mike Nests's gold chain and gold bracelets. They grabbed gold chains that guys had left with me on their way to prison or on their way out of town. Everybody thought I was trustworthy and I recall a guy saying that when he got back, I would be the only man in the world that would still have it for him and if he didn't return, I could have it. The bracelet appraised for $3,500 and I let him have $500 and held the bracelet for collateral.

They took everything in there, mine or not.

Burt Bodiford grabbed my life savings recklessly. I recalled being raided in 1975 under the suspicion of booking games with Gene Easterling. Easterling booked for football games and the government investigated. On that occasion, the agents made me open my safe and took the money. However, the agents documented every nickel and dime in my safe and gave me a receipt; I got all of my money back. Fifteen to twenty years later, I never thought the Department of Justice would steal. But in 1994, the agent in charge told them to clean my safe. Keep in mind I'm not a drug dealer. I am a schoolteacher operating a nightclub, which is very rare, I admit.

OPENING THE SAFE WAS a turning point for me, the beginning of a slide into a bureaucratic nightmare. If I hadn't opened the safe, the story would be different, I wouldn't be broke, and this book probably wouldn't have been written. The money disappeared from my house and did not find its way back.

Agent Bodiford exited my home and took me to my nightclub. I was never handcuffed. They thoroughly checked my nightclub and didn't find any drugs. They asked me to open my safe at the club and took every dollar bill they saw. This included money in the cash registers at the upstairs and downstairs bar, and the door money. They cleaned me out.

By then, WSFA-TV reporter Eileen Jones and a crew were outside my club ready to film. The cameraman held the camera on his shoulder, waiting to get a shot of me exiting my club, surrounded by law enforcement, looking guilty.

Bodiford looked out then turned to me and said, "Mr. Thomas, I know you don't want to fool with these reporters."

I agreed. Bodiford told my brother, Hiawatha Thomas, that I should be back in a few hours. Then Bodiford got into his truck and cranked the motor. He then signaled for me to jump in. I walked out of the club and jumped into the passenger side and we drove off, the camera rolling the whole time. My wife and friends later told me that I made the 6 o'clock news.

So, how did Eileen know I was going to be coming out of the club? I had only granted permission to have the club searched thirty minutes prior. I think—I'll never know for sure, but it is the only logical conclusions—that the government agents alerted the media to help build a public case against me. It was another leveraging tool to further twist the screw.

This destroyed my reputation and my business. I lost the business of those perfect gentlemen from the Air War College. There were even Saudi

Arabians that were students at Maxwell Air Force Base who attended my club and I had a good relationship with them. Some were heads of the Saudi air force. They sent for me one Christmas to come to Saudi Arabia but I decided not to go.

We proceeded to DEA headquarters. Bodiford took me on a tour of the headquarters, showing me the gambling and drug stamps. On the walls were pictures of President Bill Clinton and the Honorable Janet Reno, smiling. Four men sat at a four-by-eight table in one room, counting and arranging stacks of my money. He then told me that in about an hour or so I would be able to go back to my club. I then asked him how he thought I would be able to open my club after all my money had been taken.

"How much do you think you need to open the club?" he asked

I told him I needed between $400 and $600.

Bodiford went over to the table and got $400 and gave it to me.

Shortly afterwards, Assistant U.S. Attorney Charles Teschner approached me. "Thomas, you have more cash money than I make a year," he said. "Your home is twice as large as mine, yet you report half the income I do a year."

"Sir, as far as my home is concerned, I build houses. If you had given me the money to build your home that you paid for yours I probably would have built you one twice as large. I built Dr. McCorvey's women's medical center and remodeled Top Flight. As far as the cash money goes, I never have time to spend money. I work all the time, I don't go to the malls, basketball games, or movies. And I gamble," I explained. I had a lifestyle different from most Americans. I practically lived out of my club and the shoe shop. I like to work and used the club as a social outlet. All I did was make money and save it; I never had an opportunity to spend it. I was good at gambling; it usually brought in supplemental money. I never touched the money in my safe, except for one time. I'd lost all my daily cash in a card game and the painter who painted my home said I owed him $400. I went to my safe and paid him—that was the only time.

Teschner gave me a long stare while puffing another cigarette. He glared at me. He was suspicious. I was guilty in his eyes. I could see it. He assumed I was a black man rich off drug money. He saw a loafing criminal, a worthless Negro. I didn't think much of him either. He smoked one cigarette after another showing little to no respect for me, therefore I had none for him. I could tell right away that he was a jerk.

I told him that he had smoked five cigarettes in front of me in the last thirty-five minutes without my permission and that he looked like a drug dealer to me. I added that I would put him on a thousand dollar a year cigarette expense and after twenty-five years he would have $25,000 in his safe if he left those cigarettes alone . . . and that they were going to kill him. I went on to explain to him how much I hated drugs. I also told him that anytime I came near drugs I called Larry Armstead and furthermore the key to having money is never having the opportunity to spend it. I also said that I had much more money than he made a year if he and his department had not stolen any.

Teschner asked me again about Larry Armstead.

I reconfirmed what I said by telling him about an incident I had with a disc jockey at my nightclub. It was brought to my attention that he was doing drugs. I immediately called Larry Armstead and asked him to investigate the situation. Larry agreed to handle the situation.

"You didn't tell Larry about those three keys we took from Drayton on Super Bowl Sunday?" Teschner said.

"Three keys, what's a key?" I asked. He turned red.

"Here's my card," Teschner said. "After a good night's rest in jail you ought to be able to talk better in the morning!"

"Sir, I'm not taking your card. I've already told you the truth like I swore to Bodiford at my home."

"Well, get a good night's rest. Bodiford, take him to jail!" Teschner replied.

Bodiford never handcuffed me. I rode to the Montgomery Police Department and went to jail. During this time I'm thinking, Squirrel, this is nothing. They have the wrong guy and you'll be free in no time and you'll get your money back. I know I'm not involved with cocaine and no one can say they have ever seen me with a cigarette.

On the way to jail I remembered calling the police on my brother Buck in 1978 because I saw some mysterious buds in my ashtray at my home. After the police confirmed that they were marijuana buds, I threw Buck's clothes and belongings into the street on St. Johns. Furthermore, I didn't speak to him until my older brother's funeral, more than twenty years later.

Bodiford took me to jail and while being booked in, I was asked to empty my pockets. I turned to give the $400 back to Bodiford but he refused to accept it. The black male processing me in stated that I couldn't have more than $30 accounted for at the jail. He recognized me from Top Flight and agreed to keep the remaining $370 until the opportunity permitted me to store it elsewhere. We then proceeded down the hall. I asked the black officer where Curtis Drayton was. The officer stated that there were specific orders that didn't allow us to be together. It was probably due to the two of us being co-defendants.

The jail smelled of Pine-Sol. There were wide hallways and two parts of the jail housed the federal inmates. As we moved forward he quietly told me to stop by the vending machine and Curtis would be to my left and he would let me talk to him. I looked to the left and Curtis was in a special cell. I could only see a small portion of Curtis's face. I asked, "Curtis, what the hell is going on?"

"I don't know," he replied in a low tone.

The jailer took me into the cell with four other inmates. One of the four was Robert "Franko" Franklin. Franko was picked up around the 1st of February, 1994. I knew Franko from my gambling game. Dr. Frank Pollard brought Franko to my game as a guest. After that, Franko came to my club from time to time.

"Squirrel, I hope they aren't tying me into this shit with Flowers," Franko said. Flowers was the nickname of Oscar Andrews, a guy I had gambled with a few times.

"What in the hell am I doing down here?" I asked.

"I don't have the slightest idea," Franko assured.

We continued to mingle until I fell asleep. It wasn't a very upbeat conversation.

5

THE CASE UNFOLDS

On that Friday, Bert Bodiford took us in his truck to be arraigned. Outside, another agent asked Bodiford where he got the truck from. "Off one of them out of Tuskegee," he said.

I was issued a complaint at DEA headquarters. My name was added to the complaint after Teschner didn't get any expected information from me. He assumed I was lying. The $25,000 I received for a gambling debt from Curtis Bell was mentioned. The complaint listed everyone involved in the conspiracy.

I noticed that everything centered around a man named Michael Maye. His name was affiliated with several major drug dealings. Maye was an interesting case, and another example of the problems with our drug laws. He was a dealer from way back. While Maye was working for the federal government as a witness, he was busted for selling dope at Lee's Chicken. They paid him to be a witness, he was reporting to them at this time, and meanwhile he's selling dope. They had a trial for him and he went to prison. He was sentenced to seventeen years. So he offered testimony to the "Flowerman" case, the case I later found out I was attached to, in exchange for a commutation of his sentence.

This is my connection to the Flowerman case.

One of my buddies, Gene Easterling, played a large book with a number of high-rolling gamblers. Gene was a white fellow, a great guy, and everyone loved him. Everybody was all right with Gene. All the bankers and politicians loved Gene. He was a popular guy and knew just about everyone in the gambling world. He was one of my good friends. He was also a practical joker. One night, Gene sent his friends, who were police, to bust up our gambling game. So the police in full regalia came and led us out of the game with our hands up. I thought we were going to jail. Suddenly Gene arrives, yelling obscenities, demanding the police let us go. And he was giggling. It was hilarious.

Now Gene began running book for a fat cat in Miami named Oscar Andrews, also known as the "Flower Man." Before I started hanging out with Gene, I didn't know much about Andrews's personal life other than he stayed in Mt. Meigs, Alabama, had gone to school at Georgia Washington, and moved to Miami where he owned day-care centers. Oscar was a big-time bettor. He would punch out mid-level bookies with enormous bets and he knew sports and how to run things. I saw Andrews around and he and I never had any problems. Well, he began betting with Gene, and Gene began losing. Oscar eventually beat Gene for $95,000.

After Gene paid him, Gene got sick with a brain tumor and died. Gene had told his wife he wanted all his pallbearers to be in a limousine. I was the only black guy in the limousine as we rode to put Gene in the ground. The six of us were all bookies. I ran a small, legal book. But when big bets came my way I would send them to Gene and keep a little profit. Thomas Jordan and Bob Mason, who were also in the limo, did the same thing. So Jordan says to me, on the way to the funeral, "Squirrel, a lot of white people are wondering who's going to run the books now. You gotta help us." We talked about two things: picking up the slack now that Gene was gone, and getting some of Gene's money back from Oscar.

After the funeral we ironed out the details and I began running a small bookie business, legal, as I had less than five people involved.

"What about the black guy who beat Gene for all that money?" Mason asked.

So I called Andrews. I explained to him that I was going to fill in some for Gene with the betting. "I don't want to break you up like I did Gene," Andrews said. "Just don't fool with me this fall. I'd hate to do to you what I did to Gene. I put that tumor on him with all these heavy bets. I broke every bookie in Miami." Then he showed that much of his tough talk was just that as he sincerely asked if the large flower arrangement he sent to Gene's burial had made it.

Now, after all this, Gene's wife, Mrs. Ann Easterling, Thomas Jordan, Bob Mason, and I wanted to break Andrews. We decided to book that fall. The four of us agreed to split Oscar up four ways to accommodate all his bets. And we beat him for $38,000. After the college season, we get ready for the bowl games. The pros start playing on Saturdays. So we got Oscar to bet $38,000 down and he comes to Montgomery. He calls me and begins his scolding. "You coward; why didn't you tell me there was a game today?! You're worried about that money I owe y'all."

If you're a big bettor, and you haven't called me about a game, I'm not going to remind you. If you wake up a sleeping giant, he'll wake up and whip the shit out of you. This was a favorite saying of Gene's: never wake up a sleeping big bettor—he'll beat you every time.

So we didn't call Andrews to remind him. He got on another phone and I heard him. "Let's give that $38,000 to Squirrel Thomas in forty-five minutes." And the guy brought me the $38,000. Just like that.

Then Andrews got back on the phone with me. "Listen, you coward. I want a line on that second game. I'm going to beat, beat, and beat you," Oscar said, "and teach you a lesson on how to treat somebody—I'm gonna beat the stew out of you. You don't know how to treat a man with this betting!"

Oscar bet the second game that day that came on at 3:15 P.M. and we never beat Oscar for another game until Alabama played Miami for the national championship and Oscar bet $10,000 on Miami to beat Alabama -8 and bet $10,000 on Miami to go over 38. Oscar won the over bet but lost the Miami bet and paid us $1,000 juice. When he got through with us, he beat us for $54,000, which I paid him when Tommy Jordan, Bob Mason, and Gene's wife gave me their shares in February 1993.

We should have known better, I suppose. But this was how I knew Andrews, a big-hearted gambler who liked to talk trash. Oscar, to me, was a perfect gentleman. I never had any problem with him other than the fact of him not understanding the percentages of winning and losing the first year. He thought that if he bet a thousand dollars on a team, if he won, he knew he'd win a thousand, but if he lost, he would have to pay $1,100, a ten percent juice. After that, I never had any problems. Oscar and I also understood that we paid off when we got ready to. It wasn't a weekly thing. We kept notes of what we owed one another. Each week I would give Oscar's man, Curtis Bell, a report on where we were and add it to the balance and destroyed all records. Oscar wasn't in a hurry to pick up or pay off and the white bookies agreed that it was okay with them.

The next year, we had him $28,000 down going into Thanksgiving. Unknown to both of us, the government now had his phone tapped. They suspected his involvement in drugs. And they had me on the phone giving Curtis Bell the line. One of Andrews's men would call me and ask for the Gizmo, which meant the line. "Run it down to me," the man would say.

Every week when we straightened up, I would give every one of my bettors a new "book." We straightened up on Tuesday. The book had every game listed in the order they would play. The man looked in the book and had the game listed. He would consult his book, and I would look at my book, with the spreads on each college and pro game, and then he would call me back and tell me what he wanted, how much money on each game. I would call Tommy and Bob and tell them what we had. This was how we ran book. I tried to give Tommy and Bob two-thirds.

(After everything went down, Tommy and Bob, both white men, were left out of the investigation. This is yet another interesting example of our legal double standard.)

So the government had a wire on Andrews. A full-blown investigation. And they heard on the wire tap Andrews saying, "Take the money up to Squirrel who runs Top Flight. I got to straighten up and fly right so I can whip Squirrel. Go pay him. Then I'll start whipping him again."

Gamblers can't play if they owe money. I had just paid him $54,000 in February. So I was glad to get anything. The $25,000 was a blessing. I assumed that the money was part of the money I had recently paid him. I called Tommy and Bob and told them that the ship was in and for them to come over and get their share. The next day or two they came over and got it. Most of it went to them because Oscar started betting teasers and I was afraid of him on teasers so I was giving them most of the action on the teaser bets.

Oscar was very nice to me. He would call occasionally. Because he suffered with gout, he ate plenty of fish. He would call me from the fish market in Miami and say, "I know you serve fish on Fridays during happy hour. Do you want me to send you a case of shrimp?"

I asked him much it would cost.

He said, "Man, all you think about is money. Can't a friend send a friend some shrimp without worrying about money?"

I said, "Oscar, I just like to keep everything businesslike. I appreciate you wanting to send me a case of shrimp."

He sent the case of shrimp and we put it in the freezer and served it during happy hour on Fridays.

The government later claimed that Andrews paid me with drug money. This is how I became involved in their investigation, through a legal, albeit high-stakes sports betting game. It's a complicated connection, but also tangential and thin. Anyone who looked at the case and at my place in it should have seen right away that I wasn't involved in the drug business.

BACK AT THE JAIL, my lawyer brother, Kenneth Thomas, had received word that I was picked up and he came down there. He had bad news.

"Squirrel, I'm not going to go for this bond because if it isn't posted you may be locked up for two to three weeks," he said. "Let me get everything in order over the weekend and we'll go for the bond Monday morning."

"Man, you mean to tell me that I've got to stay down here until Monday?"

"I believe that's the best deal. You stay down here until Monday and I can guarantee I can get you out rather than missing today asking for a bond. I want to get all the people in the community to speak for you and I know we'll make bond," he said.

"The Manhattans will be at the club on Sunday," I said . . . but it was for naught.

At the jail that night, guys from Tuskegee read the complaint and they told the other guys that they didn't think anyone was going to make bond but me. They said I was the only person not associated with cocaine and if the others involved didn't win at trial they wouldn't see daylight for a long time. They assured me that I would make bond and didn't understand why

I was tied into everything. By this point, I didn't find their hopeful words very encouraging. It was a bad weekend. Still, I tried to maintain my spirits, taking solace in my pending release on Monday morning.

Unfortunately the following Monday was a federal holiday. I wasn't able to see the judge until Tuesday.

I was taken in an unmarked van down with the other guys in the indictment to the federal building. We rattled around in the back, talking.

"I thought I told you to destroy all records once we agree on an amount for that week," I said. We didn't keep the sports books around after their time was over. In light of the charges we were facing, it was a foolish precaution.

"I did," Curtis said.

"Then how do they would know how much I received in cash?"

"I don't know," Curtis said.

"Man, they must have a wire tap; they've got to have one if you destroyed the records," I said.

"Well, I destroyed the records."

"I read the complaint and if any of you all have done any drugs with Michael Maye—you are in deep trouble," I said. " It says here, on or about the certain date, Michael Maye bought this from Curtis Drayton, on or about a certain date, Michael Maye went to Miami and got drugs from Oscar Andrews. I hope this isn't true because if it is, y'all are in serious trouble."

We arrived at the courtroom. Kenneth had retained a lawyer for me, a white guy named Euel Screws. An assistant U.S. attorney came over and said, "Mr. Screws, this is not my case. I'm sitting in for Mr. Teschner. Mr. Teschner is in Miami trying to make sure Oscar Andrews doesn't make bond."

"Man, why are you all trying to put me in prison? I don't fool with any cocaine," I said.

The assistant U.S. attorney ignored me. He repeated again to Mr. Screws, "Mr. Screws, this is not my case and I'm just sitting in and I just wanted you to know that."

Joe Merriweather spoke on my behalf to Judge John Carroll and told him that I didn't use drugs, that I didn't sell drugs, and that, in fact, I hated drugs. Joe Merriweather was a U.S. marshal who gambled with me from time to time. Along with Curtis Drayton and other members of the Gentleman's Club, we traveled to Biloxi together to gamble as well as attend Mardi Gras festivities. He frequented my club as well and was a friend.

The judge assured him that I would make bond. I was asked to put my home up for bond money. My home was in my wife's name therefore I had to wait until Lucy got home from school to sign. Judge Carroll stipulated that I could not go to my club while it was open; I could only go to Top Flight when it was closed. I don't know why I was being kept from my work but I complied with the agreement.

Afterwards, Joe Merriweather directed me to a secret door that led to a private way out of the federal building to avoid the media that waited outside. It was a cloudy day, overcast and melancholy. I got into a truck I didn't recognize and then Joe had a gentleman drive me away.

He took me back to jail and the guy announced, "Thomas, all the way out!" They gave me back my clothes, my ring, $370, medicine, and my gold chain. I went home and took a long, hot shower, washing the prison smell off of my skin. I went back to the club to go to work, still wondering what was going on.

A few days went by before I had another hearing, this time an arraignment.

I saw the other guys coming one by one into court in chains and shackles wearing gold uniforms. I didn't know much about these guys because I'd only seen them at my club. Only two of the guys, Curtis and Lorenzo, had played poker with me and bet on football games. And, as I explained earlier, Oscar had bet me on football games. I'd seen Franko, as a guest of Dr. Pollard, at my gambling game and Nathaniel Salery at my club; Salery got a table on certain nights for birthday parties and rented my Hornet Grill out to his mother and father. I was glad to do so. I had also seen Ronald Landrum at Top Flight and Terry Mitchell who collected the $54,000 from me for Oscar Andrews. I also remembered selling Terry Mitchell a leather sweater when he came to pick up Oscar's payoff.

So I knew all of the people involved, but in a town Montgomery's size you tend to know almost everyone anyway.

6

THE DISCOVERY

By now lawyer Screws had gained all the discovery and evidence in the case and he asked me to read over the documents. Every time I saw my name, he instructed me to put a small piece of yellow tape on the page to mark it so that he could look it over. This was supposed to save me money. He told me initially that the case wouldn't run me over $25,000. (Don't skip ahead, but when you see the final figure you'll see why this number is so laughably low.) So I took the evidence as it came in, mountains of paper it turned out. It took me four carloads to get all that stuff back to my club.

Now I started to read the discovery. And what I found shocked me.

I read about Mason and Chappell Hill. Mason Hill is Curtis Drayton's partner at Central Auto Brokers. They are white men and I knew them because they had their Auto Brokers Christmas Party at my club every year, and they had come to the club a number of times, sometimes with Drayton. I start reading about how Chappell Hill was busted for selling drugs at the University of Alabama dormitory and he had agreed to cooperate with the government and help them bust Curtis Drayton, his brother's partner, for consideration in his distribution case. I also read that the Task Force was working with the Tuscaloosa district attorney regarding Hill.

I read that Mason Hill was caught with marijuana coming out of Loxley, Alabama, leaving Florida. I read about the Grove brothers, Michael and Thomas, who stated that they had bought drugs from Drayton. The Grove brothers stated that Mason Hill had given them cars to drive to Miami to get drugs and when they got back, Mason Hill would get half of a key to sell to people that he knew. By the way, I had now learned that a key was a kilogram. I read everything and my name never showed up in any of the interviews, not a single one. Michael Maye, one of the informants, mentioned that I was a bookie, and he thought I worked for Gene Easterling, my white buddy who died from the brain tumor. It was the only thing that any informant said about me. It was my only relationship to the case.

The Grove brothers also mentioned they had spent thousands at Top Flight and they had bought leather pants from me on one occasion. To this day I don't know how they spent thousands in Top Flight and didn't fix their teeth. I don't remember them as customers of that magnitude.

The key guys indicted with me—Curtis Drayton, Lorenzo Hughes, Oscar Andrews, Nathaniel Salery, and Robert Franklin—were perfect gentleman. Let it be known that Clifford Jones, a cooperating individual, told the U.S. attorney that Mason Hill was the controlling influence in Curtis Drayton's and Lorenzo Hughes's drug activity. Robert Franklin was very polite at my dice games, sometimes extremely, by asking if he could pick up a bet before he grabbed it—even though he placed the bet. He would ask permission from the house and I don't know if this was done intentionally to impress me or not, but he was a gentleman. I had never heard any of these gentlemen talk about drugs or where they lived nor had I been to their businesses. Lewis Williams was the only gentleman whom I played poker whose home I'd been to. His car broke down one night and I had to take him home around 4 or 5 A.M. one morning. I had never been to anyone's home, including that of my brother Kenneth or the U.S. marshal, Joe Merriweather. I was only trying to break them in my poker and dice game every night and they were trying to break me. It was a running competition, a great on-going game.

I held Curtis Drayton and Lorenzo Hughes in high regard. They visited my club, dice, and poker game regularly and never gave me any indication that they were affiliated with drugs. They dressed and spoke well. They were nice guys.

In my own case I felt I had been mistreated and assumed guilty, as if the burden of proof was on me to prove my innocence. Which, sadly, it was and is. Because the government lied so much on me, I wondered if they had also lied or planted evidence on these guys. I can't see it any other way.

If they had a wire tap or electronic surveillance (which they did), how do they put me in it? I was mentioned one time, by Michael Maye, who said he thought I was a bookie, nothing else. I came up in a few of the transcripts in what were clearly gambling discussions.

And, later, if they could lie to the grand jury on me, then I've got to think that they might have lied and planted evidence on these other men. That's the only way I can see it because in my world, Curtis, Lorenzo, Franko and Oscar were perfect gentlemen.

7

RECOUPING MY AGENDAS

My life stayed busy. Every night the club was open I would go to the shoe shop down the street and wait until it closed. I would then go back up the hill to the club, and then take care of the cash registers and other duties. This continued until early May. Shortly afterwards, an article was published in the *Montgomery Advertiser* that I had been given permission to go back to my club. I then assumed that everything was going to blow over because I knew I had no affiliation with cocaine. I phoned Mary Briers at Cloverdale Junior High to report that things were improving and brightening up. My attorney also called and stated that things were looking good. Life was stabilizing; things were returning to normal.

But I still couldn't work in my club. This was part of my deal when I made bond. It still makes no sense to me. Preventing me from running my business seemed like a punishment before I was found guilty. So every night I stayed about three or four blocks from my club and watched TV. All of my friends, at this point, were scared of me. Perhaps they thought I was guilty. Or perhaps they were guilty and didn't want to be seen with me. Or maybe they were scared. Regardless, I spent much of this time alone. Even Alvin Holmes, a state legislator and a very powerful man in these parts, stayed away.

Bill Clinton was president at the time and he had appointed Redding Pitt as the U.S. Attorney for this area. Now Pitt and Alvin Holmes ate dinner together regularly at Sinclair's, a restaurant across the street from Cloverdale Junior High. I knew Alvin Holmes well, and I even think maybe he owed me one. In 1968, I financed part of his first campaign. But now he ran from me as if I was spreading AIDS. He didn't do anything to help me.

Holmes has accomplished a lot. So on one level I understand his reticence. A black man doesn't want to create any problems with the government. You learn that when you're black. Because the government can get you on income tax evasion, illegal phone usage, a hundred different ways. And even if you're innocent, it costs you money to defend yourself. So even rich and powerful black folk have to tread lightly.

Later on, Holmes told some of my friends that he helped me, that he talked Pitt out of going after me, but I don't believe it. They got me any and every damn way they could. They tried everything they could to get something on me.

When the club closed each night, my people would call me and I would come up and do my work. I would cash out the registers and clean up and check everything out. This went on from February the 24th until the middle of May 1994. My customer base at the club plummeted, as did my profits. See, I had to prove that I wasn't a drug dealer. The honest folks who came to the club didn't want to patronize a criminal's establishment. And the shadier customers, if I ever had any, didn't want the heat that being near me or my club might bring. It was a terrible situation. I was losing money. I would bring shows in but I wouldn't have enough people show up to cover the cost of the act. I lost three houses and a restaurant trying to get the live venue to work. I finally stopped trying to bring shows to the club. I just couldn't pick up enough money at the door to pay the entertainer. The result: Montgomery lost one of the best live music venues it had ever had for the blues, R&B, hip hop, funk, and even rock. It was over.

All of my days were almost exactly the same. I left my home at the exact same time every day. I arrived at the club every day at 1 o'clock. I did repairs, cleaned everything, and made sure the machines were working, the bar was stocked. Then I would go by and look at my rental properties. I had one home that had eight tenants, each with their own rooms. The Hornet Grill was my building, too. I would check to see if anything needed painting, if boards were loose, and so on. Then I would go to my shoe shop, make sure everything was fine. Then I would take Jackson to Highland and go to the club parking lot.

Work, drive, work, drive, work, a little gambling at night. I didn't eat out at restaurants and I didn't do anything for fun. And this whole time an agent, unbeknownst to me, was tailing me. I found out later that the agents thought I was certifiably crazy, obsessed with work. I guess I am.

Sometime around mid-May I got word from my lawyer. I could now go to my club. Judge Carroll released me from that restriction. It was getting clearer and clearer to everybody that I wasn't into drugs. The big white people, whose children I had taught, were inquiring about my case in conversations at the Montgomery Country Club. It became clear that I wasn't involved at all. So the U.S. Attorney's office received more than three hundred letters on my behalf. Now none of these people spoke out publicly, but at this point I appreciated any friends I could find.

I kept reading the evidence that Screws was sending me. And I started calling Charles Teschner and Marshall Simmons, trying to get my things back. They both said they were working on that. I didn't believe them but I kept calling.

On June 10, 1994, I went outside to get my *Montgomery Advertiser*. The headlines read, "Club Owner's Drug Charges Dropped." It went on to say that the original indictment claimed that Richard "Squirrel" Thomas had five "keys" of cocaine on January 30, 1994; that I used two semi-automatic pistols while committing drug crimes; and that I had agreed to testify against Curtis Bell and Curtis Drayton—two men the government claimed were bringing multiple millions of dollars worth of cocaine into the Montgomery area. The article implied that the charges against me were dropped for my testimony and cooperation.

This was all quite a shock. Being as I was supposedly the main witness in a high-profile drug trial, I should have known something about the proceedings. I was relieved that the charges had been dropped, but the article made it seem like I was testifying to get a lesser sentence. The article presented me as guilty. The article was riddled with inaccuracies. The article ruined my life. The first amendment doesn't grant anyone the right to destroy a person's life and yet they destroyed mine.

I got a phone call that afternoon from Curtis Drayton's mother. She said, "Squirrel, I'm so happy you been cleared. Then I read that you're going to testify against my boy." I explained that I wasn't testifying against anyone because I didn't know anything. I think she believed me.

I also got calls of congratulations from friends and former students.

As the shock passed, I began to think about the article and where it came from. The task force involved many important government people, including high-ranking prosecutors and ambitious agents looking for a big collar. The article, I felt, was a way for the task force to cover up its mistakes. Instead of telling the media they made an error in my case, the task force resorted to defamation. Better to assassinate my character than end up with egg on their faces. And, if I was put in danger from people who now thought I was going to testify against them, I would have to run to Teschner for help. This is how many government lawyers work. They push you into harm's way so you'll testify for them. (I have more examples of this later.)

Or perhaps it was just bad reporting from the *Advertiser*. Lord knows they had gotten stories wrong about me before. But at the time, and part of me still thinks this, I felt that the newspaper and the government were working together against me. I wanted to file a lawsuit but my attorney, Screws, told me I couldn't sue. He said that on the Sunday in question, someone had five keys of cocaine, and since I was declared part of the conspiracy, I therefore had five keys too, until I was proven innocent. I still don't understand how that one works, but I know that it doesn't feel right. Finally, I realized that if the government and media screwed me, then they might have screwed everyone else.

I knew that I never agreed to testify against anyone; I didn't know anything. I didn't know any of these guys were involved with drugs. I knew hundreds, if not a thousand, people in Montgomery. Living in a place for most of your life yields a large community of friends and acquaintances. If I had prior knowledge of drug dealings, I certainly would have mentioned it to Larry Armstead, like I had before.

As more evidence came in, my attorney, Euel Screws, would continue to give it to me and I kept reading it. I would read the evidence when I was cooling my heels at the shoe shop during the hours while the club was open; this was before I was allowed back in my club during its operating hours.

The discovery evidence cleared up some mysteries. For instance, I finally read a transcript of the wire tap that had Curtis Bell calling me wanting the gizmo (the betting line) and I would repeat the line to him and he then would call me back in about thirty minutes and tell me how the bettor wanted to bet. This was our process and every Tuesday I would call Curtis Bell and tell him how the weekend went and we would agree to all the terms and money owed to me or to him. No money was exchanged at this time, we would make a verbal agreement, and then I would tell him to destroy all the records, because at that point we were on the same page with the previous week's betting and payouts.

I then read on the wire tap transcripts that Larry Armstead identified my voice with that of Curtis Bell when they first started the wire tap on December 13, 1993.

Shortly after that, I recalled, the white bookies had come by and told me to be careful because they had gotten word through some of the white secretaries in the federal building that a lot of FBI agents were coming to town this weekend and they didn't know if they were going to do any bookie-busting or not.

I said, "We aren't booking under federal law." He said he knew but for me to be careful anyway. Federal law states that five or more men must conspire in order for it to be considered bookmaking. What we were doing wasn't illegal.

I took the advice I was given and took some precautions. I had given my man who worked the Top Flight parking lot, Robert Blount, a cell phone in the event that any trouble started. He could call the police and get immediate help. I switched phones with him and gave him my cellular phone and I took his. I told all my bettors to call me on the new number, 224-8339. So Curtis Bell called me just like he did every Saturday morning and said, "Give me the gizmo!"

"Man," I said, "I told you not to call me on this phone! I believe this phone could be hot. I gave you a new number to call me on. The phone is tapped—they are listening." I did this so that I wouldn't be investigated under the federal gambling laws. Again, I ran a legal gambling side game, but I didn't want any trouble and I'm cautious by nature.

At some point, Larry Armstead was taken off the case. Teschner, I believe, thought that Armstead had told me I was part of an investigation. Armstead is black and I'm black and I think he was removed because Teschner was suspicious. Armstead told me his side of things a little later, in June. Something came across his desk and he contacted Marshall Simmons, head of the DEA, and was told that all of the information from then on had to go through Charles Teschner.

Armstead told me, "Squirrel, everything you said is true."

THE ENDLESS "WAR" ON DRUGS

I'm now going to talk about the War on Drugs. Now I'm not a fan of drugs. I don't use then. I never have. What I know about drugs I've read or watched on television. But people need to wake up. "Drugs" is a catch-all pejorative that includes herbs, weeds, psychotropic plants, cocaine, heroine, crack, ecstasy, and marijuana, as well as thousands of prescription pills and liquids, from Tylenol to Viagra.[1] Morphine, methadone, Ritalin, Valium, and so on are all drugs, all have side effects, and all, in various quantities, provide an altered state of consciousness, a high. So does alcohol, snuff, tobacco, and caffeine. And refined sugar, too.[2] The fact that some drugs are illegal and some aren't, that some carry much stiffer penalties than others—this is less a matter of science than agenda. We'll get into that in a moment. But first, I want to say something and be clear: the War on Drugs isn't a war on drugs at all, it's a war on black and poor people.

Drug addiction isn't a uniquely black problem, far from it. Despite what the television and news media present, whites are far more likely to use drugs than blacks. This isn't really surprising, when you think about the demographics that make up American society. Of course the majority, and an overwhelming majority at that, is going to do everything at a higher rate than the minority groups do. Even if a smaller percentage of whites in ratio to the larger society are drug users, it's still going to be a lot more people.

A pet peeve of mine is the notion a lot of people have that since the civil rights movement, this country has been a racial utopia. People believe that for the most part, everyone is now equal. Bullshit. People need to take a look at the statistics. And they need to remember their history.

Black people have always had a hard time, here in this country and in most other countries as well. And those hard times never ended. They just took different forms.

Blacks used to live in communities. People looked out for each other, even the criminals. Three things have turned many black communities into cesspools. The first is drug addiction, the ruin of families and the catalyst for petty crime. The second is the ungodly profits to be gained by selling illegal drugs. Greed has turned many young men into gangsters and thugs. This is exacerbated, I think, by glamorous depictions of gangsters and dealers in movies and music, but that's another issue altogether. The final and most damaging blow to black communities is the U.S. government's War on Drugs.

Blacks were always less inclined towards drugs than whites because black people back in the day didn't have any money. Whites did. The name of the game was cocaine. Cocaine was a white man's drug, a white powder that business types snorted through their noses to get high. Cocaine in powder form is relatively pure and expensive. It's a white man's party drug and has been popular for decades.

The inner city has a different drug of choice, although it's almost the exact same chemical composition. The word is crack. It's powder cocaine cooked with bicarbonate and crystallized into what looks like little rock candies. Crack is cheap. Crack users pay about twenty bucks for a rock they then ignite and smoke through a glass crack pipe. Crack users experience an odd delirium when they light up. Crack is stronger than cocaine, but the cocaine and crack are the same drug, just in different forms.

Now, which form do you think carries a higher prison sentence?

Crack, of course. Sentencing guidelines for crack cocaine outstrip the powdered form by 100 percent. Cocaine powder is a rich man's drug; crack is a drug of the street.

But here's a common misconception. Crack isn't just a black drug. In fact, the statistics say otherwise. Sixty-four percent of crack users are white, only 26 percent are black. Yet 91 percent of those imprisoned for crack sales are black.[3]

A conspiracy or an effect of leftover racial prejudice? That's hard to tell.

The problem with prohibition is that it empowers criminal elements by delivering enormous profits through the black market. Back when alcohol was illegal in this country, gangsters like Al Capone became millionaires overnight. The ambition of the street thug with money is limitless. Capone began branching out into other things, carrying with him the violence of the street mentality. When alcohol was legalized, Capone and his ilk lost the main source of their profits.

The demand for illegal narcotics and the enormous amounts of profits to be made from illegal narcotics have resulted in a new batch of transnational gangsters, and in a situation much bleaker than the U.S. experienced in the 1920s.

Illegal narcotics and the insatiable demand have resulted in a horrifying black market. Without government safeguards, Darwinism has empowered the worst, most atrocious, most insidious, most violent criminals; they have risen to the top. The international scope and the new technologies accompanying globalization have made matters worse, not better. A motley crew of high-tech scalphunters, murderers, kidnappers, and so on, battle with each other and governments across the globe in a high-powered, blood-soaked game. As the field is weeded of minor players, the surviving narco-kingpins ravage countries, elect officials, stab, shoot, and bomb their way to the top. It's gangsterism on an epic, unconceived-of scale. And the governments are losing.

We're dealing with an organized trans-global crime syndicate—the most ruthless band of cutthroats in the world. And they're rich. Richer than many small countries. They employ small armies, assassinate world leaders, destabilize governments and move tons of raw powder wherever there's a demand. They refuse to yield to perceived dangers. We cannot kill them all, nor can we imprison them. We'll never break the supply lines. We'll never choke off the product. There is too much money at stake. The rewards are too high.

The sad thing is, the solution is very simple. If most drugs were legalized, the kingpins of crime and their cartels would disappear overnight. Legalization, regulation, taxation, these are the things that brought the bootlegging empire to its knees. Some argue that the hard drugs—usually those with some measure of cocaine in them—are too damaging to the body politic. I agree. But look at the effect the anti-smoking campaigns are having on teenage smoking. Educational campaigns can work.

As author Gray says in his book, "The only way to destroy the black market is to underbid it."[4]

There is a systematic hubris and, well, stupidity at the core of our drug policies. Take marijuana. This is a weed. It grows on its own accord, by the sides of highways and so on. It cannot be destroyed. It has been here longer than mankind. It is a strong, durable plant that cannot be eradicated.

Marijuana—I don't use it, I'm not interested in using it—induces, from what I've read, a sort of mellow high. Marijuana is a downer. Users in the middle of a marijuana high aren't even much of a danger to themselves. Is it good for you? Not really. There are side effects to marijuana use and I won't go into them here. But why is tobacco legal and marijuana illegal? Why is alcohol legal? Long-term effects of tobacco use have been the source of a great many controversies in recent years, resulting in federal judges holding tobacco companies like Philip Morris accountable. And I don't need to even look up the statistics as to the number of drunk-driving deaths every year.[5] Alcohol kills brain cells and retards liver function. Tobacco destroys the lungs and causes all manner of long-term problems for the human body. Both cause physical impairment of some degree or another. So by what rationale is marijuana any worse?

The beginning of the war on drugs started as prohibition ended. The apparatus in place to deal with prohibition was reapplied to narcotics. The government agents didn't want to lose their jobs.[6] The early drug addict stories preyed on racial stereotypes, of either the drug-crazed Negro or the sinister opium-smoking Chinaman.[44] At the very beginning, drug propaganda relied on blacks and other minorities as scapegoats. At the very beginning, the drug war grew out of the government not wanting to downsize or get any smaller.

The first major anti-narcotics bill was passed by a bare handful of sleepy legislators more concerned with keeping to the itinerary than any drastic social change.[7] The original drug laws were predicated on a profound misconception concerning drug addiction and recovery. These influenced subsequent legislation as well as popular sentiment. The fundamental tenets informing the drug policy were: that drug addiction can be easily overcome and that addicts are inherently dangerous and criminal. Both are lies.[8] Both are still with us today, driving the average joe's thinking about drug policy.

The collective force of moral indignation, simmering through the cesspool failures of prohibition, centered on narcotics in all its myriad forms. Never mind that some drugs helped people. Worse, many drugs—addictive, harmful, or otherwise—were cleared for manufacture, but only by certain companies. So one drug would be declared illegal, the next, more harmful or not, would be cleared, all based on a commission that profited from the companies who wanted exclusive rights to manufacture one drug or another.

Money here, there, and everywhere. It's a constant theme.[9]

As with McCarthyism two decades later, self-serving politicians found great electoral power in anti-drug propaganda. Similar to the tough-on-crime speeches every political candidate makes, anti-drug speeches were a cornerstone of most politicians' campaigns. Whether the candidates themselves were drug addicts didn't matter. What mattered was the message.

At the top, it was always about power. In the 1950s, drug use was linked with subversive communist activity. A lie, of course. But it worked. The connection to communism allowed anti-drug politicians to thump the evils of narcotics, while validating the public's fears of the invisible red menace.[10] This same tactic was used to discredit various civil rights groups, such as SNCC. Their messages were undercut with allusions to drug use and addiction.

In the 1970s, the U.S. government continued exploiting drug-related fears, taking the number of known drug addicts and multiplying the number by eight.[11] Much of the drug coverage involved drug-addled kids and minorities waging war in America's inner cities. Drugs were blamed for the breakdown of many inner city neighborhoods. The truth is different. Affluent people fled the cities en masse. This flight removed much-needed tax dollars from city schools, law enforcement, and other programs. Cities, drained of economic resources, began to crumble. The middle class removed itself from the downtown areas and then began wondering why the downtown areas were in decline.

It's more complex than all this, I'm sure, but the point is that drugs in the 1970s didn't destroy our cities, people did.

Then came the crack epidemic of the 1980s. A lot of black people believe that the U.S. government introduced crack into black neighborhoods to undermine black solidarity. I don't; I think crack appeared like many new drugs and took hold. But the government's response isn't open to interpretation, not really. The drug laws became stricter.

The disastrous turn for the worse in the drug war? President Reagan's new laws of forfeiture. Now, the drug trade meant big profits for government agencies.[12] Various agencies within the government had been empowered by Reagan to steal private property. Now a mechanism was in place to fix budget shortfalls, outfit agents with the newest equipment, and fund new anti-drug programs. The anti-drug machinery became self-sustaining as long as there was stuff to steal.

Forfeiture doesn't work exactly as most people think it does. I never would have guessed that the government can take everything you own that is suspected to maybe have come from drug money. Once your things are gone, you have to figure out how to get them back. The burden of proof is placed on the accused. You have to work to get your possessions back.[13] No one helps you; there isn't a guide. The officers think you're guilty, especially if you're black, and they stand to benefit, through the money brought in by the seizures, if you are. So you have to find an attorney, and good attorneys are so rare as to be a mythical species. They also cost money, which is unfortunate because the government has already absconded with every penny you own. Most people simply lose what they have and have no way of getting their stuff back. Houses, cars, clothes, jewelry, money—it all disappears into a vast grinder and comes out the other end as harsher law enforcement.

Eighty percent of forfeiture victims are never charged with a crime. Their stuff vanishes and they don't get so much as an apology. This huge sucking machine runs on its own energy; no one knows how to escape the drug policy.

In my case, this is exactly what happened. The law enforcement agents seized my money and some other things. When they dropped the charges, my stuff was already in the government pipeline. I only had a limited amount of time to get my stuff back. When I sued to get my possessions returned, the judge kicked my case out of court, basically because some of the paperwork wasn't filed in the right order. It's robbery on an epic scale, and I'm just one of thousands of victims.

Let's take another look at the numbers I mentioned in the first interlude. Thirteen percent of monthly drug users are black. But blacks are being incarcerated at a rate of close to 10 to 1 over whites. They are twice as likely to receive prison time and the sentence will be 20 percent longer. Who would ever claim that the U.S. justice system isn't racist? Look at the numbers.[9] From 1986 to 1991, the number of African American males incarcerated on drug charges increased by 429 percent. Blacks compose about half of the prison population, but only 12.3 percent of the overall population. And even conservative estimates place white drug use at least equal to that of African Americans, while some experts argue it is much higher.[14]

Then people wonder why black people don't have faith in American justice anymore.

Mandatory sentencing is another misstep in the U.S. War on Drugs.

The mandatory minimums in federal drug cases, combined with the absence of any parole, have resulted in an explosion in long-term inmates often in jail for nonviolent crimes. Violent felons are often cycled through various jail systems faster than nonviolent drug offenders.[15]

There's an incessant need by the law enforcement of this country—and I don't pretend to understand it—to find criminals all the time, as if the proportion of criminals to regular citizens stays the same (it does not and cannot). So prosecutors will cut deals with convicted drug dealers to ensnare, entrap, or imprison suspected drug dealers. This is insane. The man in jail has every reason to lie and no incentive to tell the truth. There is no reason to believe that the convicted dealer has learned the errors of his ways in prison and much evidence to suggest the opposite, so why does he get a lesser sentence to imprison someone who *might* be guilty?

A second troubling aspect of this practice is that convicted black drug dealers are hardly ever used to convict suspected white drug dealers. In these types of cases, the black dealers are discredited immediately.

The drug policy is pushing out violent offenders to make room for nonviolent drug offenders. Even if all of the black convicts are guilty (which they aren't), violent offenders—bank robbers, kidnappers, killers, extortionists and so on—shouldn't be released to make room for new drug offenders. White-collar criminals—who milk this country for billions every year, destabilize the economy, deprive citizens of public monies intended for basic amenities—receive far less penalties than street-level dealers. I would receive a far longer sentence for carrying a pound of a naturally occurring substance than I would if I assaulted someone and maimed him or her for life. It's an incredibly deranged set of values on display.

The majority of drug users are white. But the media almost uniformly shows users as Latino or African American.[16] This is another problem, but one I won't go into it here.

Ultimately, the war on drugs has failed. It is impractical, impossible, unrealistic. Our country is too big with too many borders and the demand is too great.[17] Use is up, as are drug-related murder rates, and, of course, the costs of incarceration. We cannot continue as we have in the past. We have to try a different approach.[18] Too many innocent people, like me, for example, are caught in the crossfire.

There are some ways to right the problem:

Drug treatments can work. This is the first mental step that people need to take. If the upper echelons of government would accept this fact, then we could begin making some significant changes. Addicts can be functioning adults. Addicts don't have to be thieves.[19] Addicts often commit crimes, both petty and serious, due to the anxiety they have of not being able to get their fix. Widespread treatment programs, with real government funding, could make a huge dent in street crime. And giving drugs away to serious addicts would be infinitely preferable to running gunfights in Chicago, L.A., New York, and guerilla warfare across the world.[20]

In countries that provide narcotics to addicts, street trade has diminished.[21] With diminished street trade comes diminished profits for dealers, weakening the overall power structure of the international drug trade.

Drugs are illegal. Drugs are expensive. Drugs are addictive. These three added together equals rising crime and a rise in crimelords in the pursuit of drug profits. The answer: sensible regulation, new tax revenues, and restricted usage, à la Holland.[22]

A systematic approach should be employed in keeping young people away from drugs. It should begin in preschool. Similar tactics being used with smoking are working. Commercials, television, and film can all be utilized to cast drug use in a negative light. But honesty is needed. Kids who try marijuana and don't go on a killing spree begin to believe that they've been lied to about all drugs and often will try something harder. The glamour of drugs has to be removed.

Third, drugs have to be legalized in some form. This isn't because I'm an advocate of drug use, quite the opposite, but we need to approach this problem pragmatically. Ghetto kids are drawn into the world of drugs because they can see and smell the profits and money. Remove the criminality from the drug trade and the gangsters and thugs who are embroiled in murder, extortion, and so on will disappear; the prison system will stabilize; the national budget will level off.

Fourth, I think all nonviolent, black drug offenders should be released from prison. Too many have been shoved through an uncaring system that judged them before the fact for their skin color. Too many are innocent of their crimes. Think about how many death row inmates are being exonerated due to the new DNA testing techniques. Now think about how many more drug cases there are and have been! If even 10 percent of the incarcerated are innocent (and I think this is far too low a number) then imagine how many innocent people are behind bars.

I don't like drugs. I think they're bad for people, for families, for communities. I think drugs are bad for the soul. But the "War" on Drugs is a cure far, far worse than the disease.

8

JUSTICE OR REVENGE?

There is a fine line between justice and revenge. Many times prosecutors and cops, judges, people on the side of the law, fixate on suspects. Prosecutors sometimes become convinced that certain people are guilty, despite evidence to the contrary. When we as a society give too much authority to those in law enforcement, it makes ordinary citizens vulnerable to personal attacks. I think that we have given the government and law enforcement too much power in prosecuting drug laws.

We are no longer innocent until proven guilty. We are now guilty until we pay money to buy our innocence.

After the charges against me were dropped and the erroneous newspaper article came out, Teschner came to my home. The U.S. Marshal parked out on the street. I was in the house, asleep. My wife came and got me. Wiping the sleep from my eyes, I went to the great room to talk to him. When I saw him standing there, dressed in his suit, the man who had caused me so much pain, I got angry.

"Man," I said, sarcastically, "aren't you afraid to come alone to the home of a member of the notorious Flowerman drug ring?" I walked to the door and peeped out; the U.S. Marshal sat in the truck about fifty feet from my home. "If I were to jump you, even the U.S. marshal couldn't help you. Aren't you afraid?"

Teschner remained quiet.

I was right to take it personally. Congress has given powers to different agencies. So the DEA, for instance, has the power to investigate and to compile evidence. But the DEA cannot order an indictment. Only someone from the U.S. Attorney's office can do that. So I had the man responsible in my home and I was going to give him a piece of my mind.

"If you remember, you all went on Red Alert when Flowers came to Montgomery. Nobody could come in, nobody could go out, no visitation . . . even if you were locked up, your mother couldn't visit you. Men were on top of the jail with shot guns."

"Y'all are trying to destroy me," I said. "I don't want to talk to you until you tell me why you indicted me and didn't indict Mason and Chappell Hill."

Teschner was dismissive. "I don't really want to talk to you," he said. "I might need to talk to your wife."

My wife came in and Teschner turned to her. "Every drug ring has a brain and a banker," he said. "We tried to bust this drug ring for five years and couldn't bust it until we got a wire tap. Your husband qualified to be both the brain and the banker." He paused. "This is the way I see it." He turned back to me. "Only a brain like yours could have taught them how to evade us for five years."

I kept my temper under control. "Well, why couldn't it have been the white Hill brothers? They've got drug records. You caught them with drugs, Mason is Curtis's partner; informants have told you all that they were in charge of Curtis and Lorenzo. If you're stupid enough to believe—I understand now, you're not from Montgomery. You see, I've done my homework on you—you're out of Kansas City."

He was surprised to hear this.

"And I know you like Jack Daniels," I continued. "I'm well into you because I want to study your personality and what makes you tick. I know you like Jack Daniels, I know for a fact you're out of Kansas City, and I know you were in the Air Force and U.S. Attorney Wilson brought you here because he met you in the Air Force. I've done my homework on you and I'm going to dig up everything on you. Why couldn't it be the Hill brothers? If you are dumb enough to believe that a black man who barely finished high school in Prattville is going to be over the top white boys in Montgomery, you're crazy as hell. If there be a boss, it's going to be the white boys. Even with my bookmaking . . . you don't really believe that I went to the white boys and asked them if they wanted to bet? In the South, the white boys go to the black man. Curtis has gotten everything he needed from the Hill boys. He's on top of the world. They got a line of credit from Union Bank, go over to Atlanta and buy all the used cars they want because I've seen them at my club on Wednesday nights trying to recruit fifteen to twenty guys to go with them to drive the cars back. Curtis and Mason Hill sold me three cars."

(I should explain. I would pay Curtis $1,000 for a car and I would then tell the guys that Curtis had money and they would entice him to come to the shoe shop and gamble. This was my way of winning some of the money back because I would be cutting the game and I could play better than any of them. I liked Curtis, but business was business.)

I continued with Teschner, even though he wasn't listening. "I saw the Hill boys sell a car for $18,000 and get paid in cash. They didn't report a penny of that money. I read where the informant, Clifford Jones, reported that as far as he's concerned, Mason Hill was in charge of Curtis and Lorenzo's drug activities. And I've read where the Grove brothers told you Mason gave them cars to drive to Miami and get the dope. And I know you know from your investigations that Mason Hill was with Curtis from the time he opened the car lot up until he closed it and he went to Igor's, Capitol Oyster Bar, and Top Flight with him."

Teschner stayed still although I couldn't tell if he were listening.

I reminded him that his wire tap freed me. Curtis is quoted as saying on the wire tap in a conversation between Curtis and Terry Mitchell, "'Man, I want to go to Squirrel and see if he can find out if they've got a warrant on me [after they took the three keys from him on Super Bowl Sunday] but man, we don't fuck with Squirrel in our business and I don't want Squirrel to know I'm in this goddamn business.'" This was the quote that eventually resulted in the charges against me being dropped, according to Screws.

"Now, you heard that on the 31st of January," I said (which was an educated guess). "But on the 24th of February you indict me with your lies. If you're gonna lie, lie correctly. You destroyed me and all you talked about to the grand jury was Top Flight. The members of your jury were from Dothan, Clanton, Opelika, and almost to Selma and all they read is the *Montgomery Advertiser* and all the *Advertiser* published was about bodies lying in Top Flight and that's why you told the grand jury that I was the owner of Top Flight. And the seed has already been planted that I was the owner of a nasty, lowdown business. Which was not the case! You never mentioned I was a retired school teacher, you never mentioned that the kids dedicated the yearbook to me, the first black teacher; you never mentioned that I integrated Cloverdale Junior High, you never mentioned that I was nominated for Man of the Year against Winton Blount and C. T. Fitzpatrick, two of the leading men in Montgomery.

"If you put me in prison, do you really think it would help solve the drug problem in Montgomery? You used trickery and deceit to put me in jail. You had no evidence. I don't like any man that lies. You had no evidence against me."

I continued to give him a big piece of my mind. I told him that I didn't like Bert Bodiford, a kid who stayed with me for nine months and he never saw me go to the office to tell on another teacher, I was too busy teaching my class. He never saw me associate with other teachers, I was too busy with my students. But my years of working around students, which Bodiford witnessed firsthand, were dismissed, ignored. As if I had never given so many years to developing better students, better math scores in the county.

I told him that he didn't indict Mason and Chappell Hill and that was an injustice. Two well-known, big-time dealers and they were busy trying to bust me.

I told him that the money amount returned to me was wrong and that he said himself that I had more money in my safe than he made in a year and that I guessed he made more than $49,000 a year. "You aren't talking to a fool now," I said, "and I got a pretty good brain and I was trained from jump street on how to think and how to compete with white folk. In fact, I was trained that we were better than you all. And when they came to integrate, it was our job at Alabama State Lab to show you all. Now remember all of this because I got it all right here. Now, do you remember the first night I had more cash money than you made all year and then you all come up with this $49,000 crap."

I said I had $4,500 I made at Lundy Brothers, $4,500 selling shoe repair equipment, I hit the Florida Fantasy Five on September 26, 1990, for $48,000, all stacked up neatly in my safe. Now when I add those figures together they come up to more than $49,000. Not to mention all the money shoved in for twenty something years. I saw four men unraveling my money and counting it at DEA headquarters, the twenties, tens, and fives.

"And the problem is that in your mind, you got this money from a nigger and who is going to believe that a nigger has this kind of money. So y'all took what you wanted to take. Bert Bodiford went back and got $400 of it, handed it to me without giving me a receipt and could have easily asked for $4,000, took $3,600 and put it in his pocket and gave me $400. That's the way I see it. There is no kind of bookkeeping system.

"I held you federal agents in high esteem," I said. "I let you search my house without a warrant because I hadn't done anything wrong and I knew you weren't going to mistreat me. When y'all raided me in 1975 for bookmaking and turned out it was nothing you wanted and dropped me—but you counted all my money like gentlemen and gave me a receipt for every penny and I signed the amount you took. But you all didn't do that this time.

"No, y'all have completely ruined my life and I don't have the same kind of respect for you all whether it matters to you or not."

Teschner responded. "I'm going to order them to return everything they have taken from your home."

Of course, this never happened. Teschner left with no fanfare. Meanwhile, the government was preparing its case against all the people involved. But none of the people they indicted went over to the government, which as far as I know is pretty rare. So, this was a peculiar case. Teschner readied himself for the trial while I tried to reassemble my life.

9

COLLATERAL DAMAGE

The charges were dropped but I wasn't through with the government and the government sure wasn't through with me. I was on my way to Atlanta to buy some clothes when I got a call from my lawyer saying that the DEA wanted to interview me the next morning at 9 o'clock. I told him to relay a message: I wasn't going to meet them at DEA headquarters, nor was I going to meet them at the U.S. Attorney's office. And that my testimony hadn't changed from the first time I gave it. "Get me a motel room," I said, "and I'll meet you there. Then give me the key when we're done so I can get some rest. If y'all agree, I'll talk in the morning." They agreed.

I asked my attorney what they wanted to talk to me about, anyway.

"They just want to interview you," Screws said. "By the way, Clinton Perry would be there. Do you know him?"

"Yes," I said. I knew Clinton. He was my fraternity brother in the Kappa Alpha Psi fraternity at Alabama State University. The Kappas were formed in Bloomington, Indiana, mostly as a response to the civil rights issues going on in that state. Indiana was a racist place; they elected a KKK man for governor. Lots of famous black men have been Kappas: Bill Russell, Wilt Chamberlain, Johnnie Cochran, and Tavis Smiley are just a few. Clinton had grown up with me here in Montgomery; he was younger than I am but still someone I knew well. He was now a DEA agent out of New Orleans. I didn't care who was going to be there; it didn't make any difference to me.

I went to the hotel over on Carmichael Road around 9:30 in the morning. The same task force that had run the case from the beginning was still running things. The room was full of people: DEA, FBI, ABC, Montgomery police, and two white, female stenographers with their typing machines. Marshall Simmons was there, waiting. Agents lined the walls, sat on the beds, and lounged in the chairs. It was a packed house. I sat down, and said, "Before y'all interview me, may I interview you all?"

And I started right in. "I want you to explain to me why I was indicted when I've never touched so much as a cigarette in my life and yet these Hill boys, known drug dealers, haven't been."

I was indicted by association. So, what did those white Hill boys do? They were not only associated, they were in business with them, according to "federal" evidence. "You guys said I associated with Curtis and some of the others," I continued. "Well, if you call waiting on them at the club and playing poker with them association, then I associated with them. But what did Mason Hill do? He worked with them, he went to Atlanta with them. He went to Igor's, the Oyster Bar, and Top Flight. And these are the places I know from reading the evidence. I don't know where else they went." I paused. "So what I want to know is, why did y'all indict me and leave the Hill brothers alone?" Furthermore, why didn't you indict Bob Mason and Tommy Jordan?"

Ms. Kathy Watts with the Department of Public Safety jumped up. "Mr. Thomas," she said, indignantly, "we only had three men to give us information on Mason Hill!"

"Lady," I said, "you didn't even have one on me!"

She sat back down and didn't say anything else. The message was clear. She didn't need anyone to inform on me for me to be a suspect; they would need at least a hundred respectable white men in order to indict a white man. Clinton Perry, my old frat brother, just sat there and never opened his mouth. While they sat, arms crossed, I told them my story, again, and how I did not and would not change. I told them that I loved Curtis, Lorenzo, and Oscar like brothers and had the utmost respect for them. They have never lied or mistreated me and we could always reason out any problem we ever had. They never fought in my club and helped with a lot of fraternity fundraisers. And I told them that I think they lied on them like they did me.

Because I had spent so much time with the discovery evidence, I knew more about the case than everyone, even Teschner. So I talked and talked and accused and the ladies just typed away and it was a big waste of time. All along Clinton Perry just sat there and he didn't open his damn mouth. He was a goddamn coward.

I got a little off the chain, angry. I said, "I'm not thinking about all of this anymore. I will testify the same I always have. I don't know anything about these men with drugs. They come to my club. They love to play poker with me. They were perfect gentlemen. They never raised any sand in my club. They went to church every Sunday."

"Well," Simmons said, standing up, "we might as well terminate this interview."

"I told my lawyer that," I said. "I told you everything I knew the first night." I stood up to go. I opened the door and as I started to walk through Clinton Perry finally spoke. "Mr. Thomas, since you like to gamble, why don't you build a casino?"

I ignored him. I looked around the full room and saw all those people. I thought it was very stupid of him to say such a thing. Considering the circumstances, I thought I showed restraint by not responding. But I saw him a year later. He came down the following Thanksgiving and the Manhattans had played at the Joe Reed Acaodome. He came over and spoke to me, I don't remember exactly, some small talk. And I turned to him, face to face, and I said: "I can't stand a black man like you."

My other brother, John, who worked for the U.S. Department of Interior, later explained why Perry had been involved at all. "They always tried to get people who knew people when they were younger. To help determine if they were telling the truth or not."

"But he knows me," I said.

"He was probably close to a six-figure salary and he wasn't going to risk that fooling with you."

"So that's how it works, huh," I said. "You're telling me that I have to look out for myself. Man, I can't live my life like that."

10

THE CULTURE OF RACE

Perry is just another of these black fools who has little integrity and no loyalty. See, I now understand some black men. Most of these guys wanted favors out of me, but when I needed them, they disappeared. Black men immediately understand the power dynamics of any situation. You could drop a black man into any city and by the end of the first day he's capable of knowing some of the high-powered black and white folks by name. I knew a lot of people in my day. And people wanted to be around me.

Nowadays, I don't want to meet any black men like Perry and I don't want to know any black men like him. I called them fiddlers. Remember that show *Roots*? Fiddler always sided with the boss. He wanted things to stay the same. Holmes and the others were fiddlers.

I don't want to keep returning to race but it is an essential part of my story, not just because I'm black but because others see me as black.

Whites and blacks see things in different ways. This should come as a surprise to no one. I saw on television just the other night, a rapper with a song called, "Stop Snitching." And the interviewer asked him, "Wouldn't you report a terrorist cell if you were living next to them?"

And he looked her in the eye and said, "No, I'd just move. The police are my enemy."

This is the black criminal mentality, the nigger mentality. Many black guys in the projects thinks the police are the enemy. They're raised to think this. They hear about brutality and indifference and they see the horrid surroundings and they see the police, white or black, as the problem.

I'm educated and I think the police are my friends. The police are the only thing between a thug and me. But some blacks have the criminal mentality. I played poker with some guys like this.

Now my language might bother some but I'm sixty-five years old and at this point in my life I can only tell it like it is. I've lived in Montgomery most of my life and I guess I understand it as well as anyone and better than most. Blacks live here, whites live here. A lot of people have too much money and lots more don't have enough.

Many blacks think all white authority figures are evil. But not all blacks think this way. But, most whites see all blacks as part of the same group. This is an important point and it figures in to why I had so much trouble getting out of the charges.

See, Teschner claimed he didn't hear the tape of Drayton saying I wasn't involved. He had no witnesses saying I was involved. The man in charge of Montgomery police narcotics enforcement, Larry Armstead, kept telling everyone that I wasn't into drugs. But Teschner didn't believe him, because he thought that all blacks look out for each other. Which is ridiculous. Because of the disparity in our society, especially in the South, between blacks and whites, blacks have to work harder to keep their jobs. A black police officer acts very different than a white one. You can screw up in Montgomery and become chief of police in Greenville if you're white. I've actually seen this happen; screwheads lose their jobs here and go on to become big shots in other parts of the state. But you screw up in Montgomery and you're a black officer, you will lose your job.

Here's some other examples. I taught first at Houston Hill, an all-black school. Then I taught at Cloverdale, an all-white school. When integration took place, I think it didn't do much for black kids. See, the black kids didn't learn anything from the white kids, but the white kids learned everything good from the black kids. The black kids acted like clowns. They had waltzed through school for so long and they had chips on their shoulders and they acted out. What they needed was a teacher like me who'd beat their ass with love and affection and teach them. Actually teach them. But if you don't get them young, they come out of a different mode. At Cloverdale, I couldn't handle the black kids.

At Houston Hill, I'd take a boy out to the bathroom and get right in his face. And I'd say, "I'm gonna whip you or you're gonna whip me. And you're gonna bring pencils and sit in class and do right. And you're gonna wanna fight me every day, but you'll get tired of wanting to fight me. And you'll realize I ain't giving up and you have to fall in." And the kids learned to respect me. And they would eventually do right. I was tough but I loved them, everyone.

Cloverdale was different. We couldn't do that there. And the white teachers would come over and beg me, "Mr. Thomas, will you help me?"

And I would answer, "Sure." Then I would ask, "Is he crazy to you?"

"Yes!" they'd say.

"Well, he's crazy to me, too!"

The biggest problem with most whites is they don't know the difference between blacks and niggers. Most whites put all blacks in the same boat. I don't know about Cajuns in New Orleans. I don't know about Russians in Russia. And I don't know about whites in Arkansas. I do know the difference between Judge Perry Hooper and some white man in Chisholm. They're both white, but they act different, talk different. Blacks don't put all white folks in the same boat.

Now all of this misunderstanding wouldn't be so bad, except the average black man gets hurt when he stumbles into trouble with the law. I talk about this in the interlude chapter but it bears repeating: black men do all the time for drugs. They are just a small percentage of the actual sellers and users, they don't have the infrastructure to import the drugs, but they do something like 85 percent of the prison time.

There are all these little laws that are ignored until they are used against a black man. For instance, in Alabama it is an automatic five extra years in prison if you're caught selling drugs within a thousand yards of a school. But Chappell Hill was caught selling drugs in the dorm rooms at the University of Alabama, and went scot-free.

Ignored laws cut against black people all the time. It's similar to the long period of segregation, where one half of the society had one set of rules, while the other had to live by a harder set. Now things have come a long way, I'm not going to argue that. But I always think about numbers first. It's the mathematician in me. Everything comes down to numbers. I think this is true is society, history, sociology. We had more racial problems in the South because there were more blacks living here. Now, as more Hispanic immigrants migrate to parts of the U.S., we're seeing racial unrest, as well as more Hispanic politicians, actors, and musicians.

It's difficult being a black man, but it's impossible being a poor black man. A tactic many, if not all, U.S. attorneys use is to push for the maximum sentence. This is legal intimidation. The desired outcome is this: suspects are so scared by the possibility of being found guilty and serving the maximum penalty, they either plead guilty and take a lesser sentence, thereby losing their constitutional right to a fair trial, or they cooperate, offering evidence against other people involved. And if a poor sap is innocent, he or she will take the lesser sentence and save the state the cost of a lengthy trial. The catch is this: a poor man with bad representation (which is very, very common) will say anything to get out of the maximum sentence. A poor man cannot afford decent counsel. A poor man, if uneducated, too, often doesn't understand what he is being accused of or why. A poor man will often do anything to avoid long stretches in jail. A poor man receives less fairness than the rich.

Poor white suspects are given more leeway than poor black suspects, but they have it tough, too.

So numbers have meaning, value, outside of pure math. The numbers don't lie; they can't. Examining what a set of numbers means takes a lot of time and smarter men than me. But I will say this: the disproportionate number of black men being incarcerated in this country, the actual numbers themselves, are more than just alarming. The numbers are downright terrifying.

And the major difference, the major signifier, is race. So it is, despite a lot of people not wanting to talk about it, a black and white thing.

11

Unfair Consequences of Truthfulness

After the DEA interview, I tried to return my life to normal, while still working to clear my name and to get my belongings back. Besides running my club and other side businesses, this took up most of my time.

They found the club books, a camera, and minor things of little value. No jewelry was found and only $49,000 of the $169,000 was recovered. A lot of things were missing. They couldn't find Sylvester Harvey's ring, my antique pistols, an old coin collection, or my gold chains. Most things missing were expensive and they had been misappropriated.

They did have my books for the Top Flight Club, probably to see if I had been laundering money. I imagine they looked to see if Flowers was in there somewhere. They didn't find anything in the books. I looked at the agents with their hands in their pockets, their empty faces, their nonchalant attitude of losing my things, and I told them they were liars and thugs.

Bert Bodiford told me that he was going to get all of my things back to me. I would wait but never hear anything. Then I would once again contact Bodiford or other people on the case. Promises would be made, but nothing would come of it. This has gone on for years.

Of course, I never got my property back. I made phone calls. I wrote letters. I finally spoke with Marshall Simmons, the head of the DEA, about it and he said he was going to do something. But the statute of limitations ran out. So I filed a motion to Judge Myron Thompson to get my things back and he gave me a twelve-page letter explaining my rights.

The giant paper snake, that slick, red-tape government bureaucracy with its myriad licenses to steal, has devoured my stuff and it will never be found.

The government absconded with my possessions and makes no attempts to rectify the loss, nor does it offer any excuses for itself. My antique pistols, my gold chains, some cash: it's all either in a unmarked box somewhere, locked away in a cabinet, or garnishing some agent's dining room wall. I found out later, in my reading, that I was relatively lucky. Some have everything they own stolen—the term used by the government is "seized"—never to have any of it returned. And this in cases where the charges were dropped.

The names on the indictment stayed the same and their trials were coming up. Oscar Andrews, Terry Mitchell, Curtis Drayton, Lorenzo Hughes, Dennis Price; Ronald Lang; Geraldine Frasier (she had a baby with Oscar. At one point she picked up a seafood package and took it to the restaurant. Later, the dog sniffed the box and they said it had drugs in it.); and Ben Bozman. There were others.

Teschner was still working on me as one of his potential witnesses. He asked me to come to his office over the phone. I responded, "Sir, I said I told you everything I knew on February 17, 1994 and my testimony does not change. Flowers, Curtis, and Lorenzo are the nicest guys I met. We betted on football games and Curtis and Lorenzo shot dice with me. They were church-going men on every Sunday."

Teschner asked me to come in again. "Are you going to try and coach me into lying for you?" I asked.

"No," he said.

I then reemphasized my relationship with the three men and said nothing had changed. Teschner decided not to subpoena me for the court because I had nothing good to say for him to win the case. But my involvement with this case and these people wasn't over.

In November of 1994, nine of the indictees went to trial. This included Oscar Andrews. This was the first of a number of trials associated with my case. I still didn't have my things back and was working to salvage my good name.

Oscar hired this slick, big-shot lawyer named Frank Rubino. To give you a clue as to his stature, Rubino defended Panamanian President Manuel Noriega when charges had been brought against him. He had even been on *60 Minutes* because of the Noriega case. He called me one day and invited me out to his apartment. He was staying in the Azalea Apartments behind the Mercedes-Benz dealership. I met with him and explained that I wanted to clear my name, in the open, and I wanted to help my friends. But, I said, I would only tell the truth. I didn't know who was a drug dealer and who wasn't. I wanted a record of how shabbily I had been treated. "I want to clear my name," I said, "and it is important that you ask me questions to clear my name out of this drug mess. I don't want to be associated with drugs." I thought that this might put reasonable doubt into the minds of the jury. If the government mistreats one person why wouldn't it mistreat another? I reminded him that I would only tell the truth. Rubino said that was all he wanted. I left thinking we were on the same page.

So, the trial began. As a witness, I had to stay sequestered. I couldn't enter the courtroom because I might somehow match my story to one of the defendants or other witnesses. But, the law enforcement agents were allowed to sit in and listen to get their stories straight.

I was finally called to the stand and I raised my right hand and swore on the Bible and then I sat down and waited. Now Rubino begins to ask me questions, but he follows a strange line of reasoning. The DEA task force when they went to my club had taken some of my gambling records. When they went to Andrews's apartment, they took his gambling records. And the government was trying to say these were his drug records. And Rubino was asking, if the records from Andrews's books looked like mine. I was shocked at his line of questioning. And I said yes, they looked like my books and could be gambling records. He then sat down and asked no more questions. This made me angry with Rubino because he didn't ask me about how I was treated.

Still, I destroyed Teschner on the cross-examination. I had the whole court laughing. I started crying. "They're evil," I said. "Those people will indict anybody." I only spoke the truth.

So Teschner called for a recess. "Your Honor, since it's close to lunch, we request a break for lunch." And we left the courtroom. When everyone came back, Teschner brought out all the guns he had taken from my safe and my home, making me look like a thug. Once again, my money couldn't be found anyway, and my jewelry and other valuables were missing, but anything that might help the government always seemed an arm's length away. He tried to discredit me as a witness with the guns. But one of the defense lawyers brought up the real reason. A lot of guys brought me things—guns, jewelry, rare stuff, anything valuable, really—and asked me to hold their things while they traveled, went to jail, whatever. A lot of these guys never came back. So over the years I had collected a fair number of guns, along with other belongings. But it was all legal and I had never used any of them.

By the end of the trial, all of the indictees were found guilty except two. One of them was in prison at the time, so the jury rightly reached the conclusion that he couldn't have been involved. The other guy, Dennis Price, a friend of mine and the nephew of Judge Price, had a hung jury. There would be at least one other trial.

By the way, the pistols that Teschner showed during the trial, I never got them back. They disappeared into the ether with my money and other valuables.

Lewis Howard, on his death bed, told his wife, Eliza that the government said they would offer him a deal if he would lie on me.

12

TRIAL NUMBER TWO

Second trial. The defense lawyer called me to the stand. I met with Price's lawyer before the trial. I said, "If you're gonna represent Price, let's do it and free him. But if you are wanting Price to plea guilty, I don't want any part of it. So tomorrow you question me correctly."

Price, who I often called Fox, wasn't picked up like the rest of us. Every time they dropped somebody, everyone had to be arraigned again. It's called a superseding indictment. He was in Biloxi and he found out over the phone that the police were looking for him. So he came in and gave himself up.

So on Saturday I go to the trial with my waiter outfit on. I wanted the jury to know that I worked—red bow tie, white shirt. The lawyer came on with it. "Mr. Thomas, you introduced the modern way of teaching mathematics to Montgomery at Houston Hill?"

"Yes, sir."

"Your supervisors asked you to teach every teacher how to teach the modern way?"

"Yes, sir."

"And they were so impressed, they transferred you to Cloverdale?"

"Yes, sir."

"You were voted favorite teacher eighteen of the twenty-two years you were at Cloverdale, is that correct?"

"Yes, sir," I said.

"You were nominated and ran for Man of the Year against C. T. Fitzpatrick and Winton Blount?"

"Yes, sir," I said. "But Mr. Blount beat me out."

"Are you involved?"

I didn't answer the question and proceeded to say, "You people will indict a ham sandwich!"

The judge screamed at me, "Answer the questions, yes or no." He lost respect in my eyes. Everyone gets to talk a blue streak except the people who deserve a chance to be heard. He stopped me from saying my full piece. In fact, I even asked him to take the sign down, of equal justice under the law. "You should take that sign down," I said.

"Mr. Thomas," he said, "were you originally indicted in this case?"

"Yes, and I don't know cocaine from salt. I'm still confused and I don't know to this day why I was indicted," I said.

"Mr. Thomas, was there ever any evidence of you fooling with drugs?"

"No," I said. "And I'm cleaner than anybody over there at that table," and I pointed at the prosecution. "Those people over there are evil. They'd indict anybody. And I know I'm cleaner than Mr. Teschner. I know he smokes."

"Mr. Thomas, how long have you known Dennis Price?"

"Eighteen years," I said.

"Have you spent much time with him?" he asked.

"Yes," I said. "He would come and play poker with me from 6 in the evening until 10 the next morning. We played a regular poker game."

"During that time, did Dennis ever give you any indication that he was associated with drugs?"

"No," I said. "He was always too busy trying to win money or go to the rest room."

Once again, I defeated the prosecution on cross-examination. I'm an animated guy and I got into it. I think, or I'd like to think anyway, that my testimony helped old Dennis because the jury eventually came back with a not-guilty verdict. And that night, at the club, Dennis Price came into my club. It was great to see him, a free man. He ordered a triple shot of Hennessey. And then said, "and anything you want."

We discussed the trial and the testimony. Teschner tried to trick me. See, we had several nicknames in our network. I called Dennis, Fox. But I called two other guys Fox, too. The prosecutor asked about Fox and tried to get me confused as to which friend named Fox I meant. He was for sure confused as which Fox was which.

Man, it was great to see Price free and clear.

13

THE GOVERNMENT SCREWS ME AGAIN

Two weeks later Teschner called my lawyer. He was mad. He told Screws that he had missed Dennis, and that my testimony had messed up his trial. Because he was the top dog with all of these cases, Teschner was responsible for everything. Any slipups stopped with him. And now he was holding me partially to blame for Price getting away. It doesn't matter that Price was innocent, no sir. And it was obvious that Teschner blamed me. The pathological fixation on certain individuals seems a character trait of some federal prosecutors. I felt then and still feel that Teschner wanted to ruin my life. I told the truth during the trial. My protestations, the evidence—these didn't matter to him. He wanted blood.

During the trial, Teschner was a slick operator, too, talking about saving all our children from drugs, and almost dancing around that courtroom.

"Squirrel is going to have to answer to a gambling charge," Teschner said to my attorney. Then he explained further. I had, it seems, given a football line over the telephone.

"That ain't no damn law," I said to Screws when he relayed the information. "Everyone does that."

"Yes," Screws said. "It is."

Here are the details: before all the Oscar Andrews drama went down, I had run the tiny little football betting group, as I mentioned before. Well, over the wire, I had transmitted some football scores. The same thing ESPN, CNN, and millions of individuals do every day. This broke some law that no one ever gets punished for. I thought I was safe, because I didn't take bets across state lines, and I hadn't broken any gambling laws that I knew of. And then this shit. It was obviously Teschner getting his revenge.

So they were going to take me to trial. I asked Screws what this meant and he said I was facing two years in prison and a fine.

"With your record," he said, "you'll probably just get probation and then pay out the ear."

At this point, I knew in his eyes I was a nigger. I realized I was a second-class citizen. Justice means "Just us." In Montgomery, "Just us," means: "Just us middle class white folks." For giving a score from the newspaper over the phone, I was facing two years. Two years!

However, I thought about it. I was raised right. I was raised that if you did something wrong, if you broke the law or whatever, even if you didn't know it was wrong, you had to pay up and face your punishment. So I told Screws I was pleading guilty.

Screws pleaded me guilty and Teschner set up a sentencing date. The date was set for a weird time, the same day that O. J. Simpson's trial results were brought in. My sentencing was pushed back until 3 P.M. so that the court officers could watch the verdict.

I went down before Judge Myron Thompson, the only black judge down there. Before he sentenced me, I looked at him and said, "Your honor, will you please make Teschner and his assistants let the people of Montgomery know I'm not a drug dealer." He didn't even look up at me. Instead, fined me $17,080.30, three years probation, and a hundred community hours. And all this from the court for reading lines from the newspaper over the phone. I was truly amazed how the court allowed the white detectives to lie in drug cases.

I was given thirty days to pay $10,000, and then another thirty days to pay the rest. I went and got the money out of what I had left in my savings account at the bank. The government had now hosed me out of close to $180,000. At least this latest batch of cash was taken from me semi-legally.

A strange thing happened the next week. That following Monday morning, I got call from the court clerk. I was asked to come to the court at 9. It was 8:35, so I rushed, threw some water on my face, jumped in some clothes, and headed over. I thought the court had changed its mind, or maybe that it was going to lessen its fine.

Neither happened. I got there and the court said, "I wanted you to know, I didn't fine you $17,080.30. I only fined you $10,000. The other $7,080.30 was for your probation."

So I said, "Thank you," real sarcastic. I then received the names of some places I could do community service. I looked over the list and decided on the Food Bank. So I went over to the food bank, looked around, and decided to work there. And they loved me there. I said I'd do four hours a day, twenty hours a week. And I worked every minute of it. I was the only federal prisoner there; the other volunteers were from the state system. And they loved me too, just loved me. They called their girlfriends saying, "I'm on the line with the owner of Top Flight. And he's the nicest guy you'll ever meet!" So each day they asked me to stay and eat lunch with them. The cook would come around and ask what I wanted, and he was a good cook. I ate pork chops and baked chicken—they had everything. I loved it. They blew me up, paid me compliments, they thought I was something. I'm a freak for that kind of attention.

My job involved the canned goods that were donated. There are a lot of strict rules about what can be given to people and what can't. You'd be surprised as to how many people just dump their old food on you, though, when you work in a place like that. You don't accept a can that's bent on the seam, and you don't accept a can that's bent on the top. So we put those in a separate bin for hog farmers who would buy from us. The good food we put aside and sold or gave away to people who needed it.

The guy in charge liked me so much he said he was going to call the court and request that I be given fifty more hours. It wasn't a bad time or a bad place, working at the Food Bank.

Once my required hours were over, I did 32 additional hours but never went back. I like to help people. I voluntarily did thirty-two extra hours. And I had my own businesses to run.

14

THE THIRD TRIAL

The third trial was against Melvin Starks, and about thirteen other guys with Melvin. This was supposed to be the second trial of the "Flowerman" crew, but the Dennis Price hung jury had thrown a kink in Teschner's plans. Melvin was supposed to be second-in-command under Andrews.

I knew Melvin from the club, but I didn't know him well. He didn't gamble so I only saw him ordering drinks at Top Flight, and he sometimes bought clothes from me. So we were friendly but that was about it.

I had nothing to do with this trial and didn't want to have anything to do with it. I was still trying to get my stuff back from the various departments.

But when they got ready to try Melvin, they subpoenaed me. Bert Bodiford and another man came to my home to issue the subpoena. Believe it or not, the marshal looked at the floor of my home with distaste. He was jealous of what I had. My house is nice. I worked on it myself, but I also got lucky. Back in the day, I negotiated a contract for my friend to build a dentist office. My friend planned it all out and handled everything and then he bought too much marble for the job. So, later, he came over and said, "I'm going to give you a hell of a house present." We broke the marble up and put it down in pieces all through my home. It looks like a millionaire's floor.

After all I had been through, I wasn't in the mood to play nice. "What the hell you subpoena me for?" I asked. "You didn't even subpoena me in my own case?" They had indicted me and messed my life up so I didn't have anything but hate in my heart. "Y'all should be ashamed of your selves. You tell Teschner I might come and I might not." With that, they left.

Monday I didn't show up. Tuesday I didn't show up. Wednesday, Screws called and woke me up. "Teschner is going to get you on contempt of court," he said. I thought something wasn't right, as I didn't know anything at all about Melvin Starks.

So I went to the court. And all Teschner did was put me in the witness room. All the witnesses are kept separate so they can't hear all the other testimony and I was getting used to this as this was my third trial. It was boring, just sitting there.

Then during lunch break, Teschner played his hand. He had two U.S. marshals escort me, as if I needed the protection, all the way to his office on court square. The defendants' parents, girlfriends, and friends were all outside for the break. They see me being led by these two guards and they start in on me, yelling. They were springing. "You snitching black motherfucker. You black bastard. You son of a bitch." This combined with the earlier report in the paper made me look terrible. "You with them motherfuckers," they said. I walked by quietly; I couldn't say anything. I was paraded like I was both guilty and under protective custody. I realized then what Teschner was doing: he was trying to get me killed. He wanted me in danger, so that I would have to run to him. This is the devilishness of Teschner and many U.S. attorneys. "You're working with those motherfuckers. You black motherfucker!" they yelled.

His office was a few blocks away and when I got there, I got on Teschner's ass. "You crazy or something?"

He didn't say anything. He knew what he was doing. He knew he wasn't going to put me on the stand. He wanted to scare me so I wouldn't testify for the defense. It's an old trick, and in the movies it's usually associated with the bad guys, intimidating witnesses. He had no reason to bring me there and with no explanation and really no words at all he sent me back.

From then on, I was on precarious ground. I had to go to my nightclub with everyone in town thinking I was a snitch, that I had been guilty and then I turned state's evidence to cover my own ass. The very next night, someone fired a bullet into my club.

I went back to the courtroom and waited and the trial ended and he never called me. I heard that during the trial Thomas Grove, one of the Grove boys who said they had been given cars to drive to Miami to get drugs for the Hills, broke down on the stand. Supposedly he said, "I'm tired of risking my life and lying for the government." It didn't matter.

The trial ended with Melvin Starks, Cecil Rhodes, and Mr. Lyons, an old man that Andrews hung out with, being found guilty. The others were found not-guilty, with court-appointed lawyers. Starks had Susan James, the same lawyer who defended Don Siegelman earlier this year. Starks got life in prison; Cecil Rhodes and Mr. Lyons got about twenty-eight years each. It goes to show you: hiring a high-priced attorney doesn't guarantee a win.

By the way, Melvin, finally, has filed the right papers and he's on his way out. They didn't have anything on him. They had scant evidence, if any, and no eyewitness testimony, nothing. So Melvin only lost about twelve years of his life just for living.

15

THE MONEY TRAIL

As I said before, I never saw my money again. Here's how the money of mine they did admit having ended up never making its way back.

Teschner tricked my lawyer. Or they had a side deal which sounds crazy but they were both white and they were on a friendly basis. I knew, when my attorney called Teschner "Charlie," that I was screwed. Being a black man in the Heart of Dixie, you begin to get a certain feeling when things aren't going your way. So he and Teschner had some sort of deal, that made sense at the time, that the government would take two thousand dollars from me, and he would pay me two thousand later. During the various legal wrangling, the government prolonged the process so my bill went up. This is a common tactic: bankrupt people into submission. I'm not making this up. The government attorney has many tools at his or her disposal and most won't hesitate to use them: fear, intimidation, bankruptcy, harassment, all at the taxpayer's expense.

Anyway, Screws charged me $200 an hour or something. At the end of everything I ended up owing him $43,000. The pity of it is, he didn't do much. I went through all the evidence, I made all the phone calls and I never went to trial, no thanks to him! And I had to pay him $43,000! That's a lot of zeroes for a whole lot of nothing.

When he said he would charge me a little less, I said okay.

According to the drug laws, when Bodiford took the money from my safe, he was supposed to count the money in front of me and then I would sign saying they took X amount. This is the law enforcement officer's responsibility, not the suspect's. Bodiford and the other agents took all my money, about $160,000, and claimed it was $49,000, then dropped me from the drug conspiracy charges. The government didn't give me a receipt and there was never a record of the money they took. If readers take nothing else from this book, if you're ever in this situation, make sure the money is counted in front of witnesses and you get a receipt.

When the case concluded, I went to Screws to settle my debt. Interestingly enough, my expenses owed to him totaled $43,000 plus an additional $2,000 he'd given to the government without my permission—just under the $49,000 the government inaccurately reported they'd taken from me. Screws handed me the bill and stated that it looked as if I wasn't going to come out of this case with anything, therefore he would give me back the $2,000 he allowed the government to take. Unaware of the significance of the $2,000 at the time, I walked away with $6,000.

I continued to try and get my things back. I filed a lawsuit, this time without Screws. I didn't use Screws this time because I had paid him $43,000 for nothing. He didn't do anything. My name was dragged through the mud, my belongings were pilfered, and he charged me like $200 an hour. I tell everyone I know, now, If you're innocent, don't get a lawyer. You pay and pay for basically nothing, a piece of paper framed on the lawyer's wall.

So I went with this jailhouse lawyer, which was a mistake. I had heard about this guy they called Buffalo, a half-Indian guy, and I hired him to do my paperwork for me. I went through all this just to have Judge MacPherson, a black girl I went to high school with, turn my suit down. It turns out that Screws, as my representative, forfeited $2,000 of my money by allowing the government to seize it. This occurred without me being informed of anything. By signing the $2,000 over, he was admitting, on some stupid governmental level, my guilt. I was totally unaware of this tactic and was blindsided by the ploy. And in so doing I had compromised my attempt to get my money refunded. It's wheels within wheels, trying to get absconded money returned. Without a receipt for how much money that had been taken from me, I didn't have any hard proof. It was my word against the big bad government's and I was a black man in the white world and I was screwed. But I didn't give up.

Time was passing. I was rebuffed by everyone I spoke to. Either people were busy, or they promised to get my belongings back to me right away.

Well, Louis Farrakhan was set up to speak at Carver High School and the state (I don't know who made the decision) had stopped his coming. So the ACLU, in a public case, had sued the state. I followed the case and recognized one of the names of one of the lawyers. I called the ACLU the next day and left a message.

"If this is Eight-ball Shannon, this is R. Q. Thomas, from Cloverdale. Please call me." And I left my number.

The next morning the phone rang, and I answered. "This is 8-ball Shannon, I'm looking for R. Q. Thomas."

I said, "This is he."

She said, "I thought you needed me. I went to Yale and I used to talk about you, my first and favorite black teacher. What you need me to do?"

I said, "I've filed a suit against the government and Judge MacPherson has turned me down. Could you look it over?" She told me to bring everything to her. I delivered everything I had and she looked through it all. She then called two weeks later and explained: "You have a good case. But who ever wrote this up for you didn't cite the right cases. If I had been with you we would have tore their butt up."

Three or four years passed. I kept calling them, Marshall Simmons and some of the others. I kept calling them. Simmons sent me a vibe that he was sorry what happened to me. He said, "Our investigation didn't show that you were in drugs. But it did show that you were in gambling. But we don't indict. We collect evidence. All of it. Then we turn it in. That's our job. The U.S. attorney's office handles the indictments."

"And the Hill boys?"

"Squirrel, we don't indict. We just collect evidence."

He was telling me who was responsible. We had this conversation all the time. I always returned to the original point. Fine, y'all made a mistake with me, I don't like it but I can live with it. But how do y'all arrest me and let the Hill brothers, known drug dealers with a mountain of evidence against them, go free?"

The government kept saying they would give me my belongings back. I kept calling. I wrote letters. This went on for years. I kept thinking, these are the feds, eventually I'll get everything back. Then, the statute of limitations ran out. And I realized, they weren't going to give me anything back.

Judge Thompson wrote me a letter. He tried to explain some things but his letter was full of misinformation, I assume he got this from the U.S. attorney's office. The government told Judge Thompson that my things were seized on or about the 24th. The first lie. They seized my things on the 17th. But once I was indicted on the 23rd, on drug conspiracy charges, my belongings would have been fair game on the 24th. (Which is unfair and immoral, too, since I had been exonerated.) This was an interesting lie, designed to cover someone's ass. The letter also mentioned how I had been incriminated on a phone conversation with a known drug dealer. This also never took place. Sure, I had spoken with some of the suspected dealers on the phone, but it was always obvious what we were talking about: cards and football.

I didn't pay too much attention to the letter. I had figured out a lot. Judges and Assistant U.S. Attorneys, they're all part of the same business, a complex system that appears to be impartial and divided, but is really a big club. They drink together, they see each other every day, they probably throw parties for each other. Over time the attorneys begin to notice what judges like to hear, what kind of evidence is prudent and so on. So clever attorneys—and I'll insult Teschner all day but I have to admit the man is an attorney and he is clever—learn how to try a case in front of a judge. They become experts. Teschner knows the court. He knows how to present a case to Thompson. The defense is seemingly at the mercy of the prosecution, particularly when the prosecution uses clever, immoral tactics to indict innocent victims. Case in point: my attorney Screws and his handling of my situation. I paid him out the ear, only to be stolen from. The court and DEA Agent Clinton Perry broke my heart. I watched as Charles Teschner used the same black witnesses, case after case, but never used them to prosecute a white man. Redding Pitt fired Teschner two years after he ruined my life and there was never any media or explanation as to why he was fired. However, I'm sure I have an idea. Furthermore, Burt Bodiford was fired by Sheriff D. T. Marshall. These were the kind of people who were in charge of prosecuting me.

16

In the End

When I was dropped from the case, they added Jerry Artis to the superseding indictment. Artis was never caught with any drugs, but a convicted drug dealer said he drove to Montgomery with Artis every week and picked up a kilo of cocaine for over three years. He never spent a night in jail and only had parking and traffic tickets. Artis was innocent, but also a good guy.

He got life in prison.

Curtis Drayton, was a nice, easy-going guy I shot dice with and played cards with. A nice enough guy: he got life in prison.

Franko, who I only knew a little bit, got life in prison.

And the Hill boys? One, who was in possession of cocaine in the dormitory of the University of Alabama, the other who drove truckloads of cocaine and marijuana across state lines, were up and down involved in the drug business with evidence to prove it, the Hill brothers, what happened to them? They didn't get a day in jail.

And me?

My life is about the same, only I have this dark pit of anger and distaste, a sense of persecution, and sense of unfairness, this thick rage that I just can't let go of. I still run my club, every day I'm up there, although for all the reasons given in this book attendance is still down.

Montgomery's downtown is still a bit slow. They've tried to revitalize it with all sorts of things but the fact is, after the Bus Boycott, rich white folks fled and they did not come back. And the black community, that thrived not two miles from Court Street, they paved through it with an interstate and locked up half the black men in jail. Returning to numbers, that is a pattern; the governments have done this in dozens of Southern cities.

No, I'm not unhappy, but I'm not happy either.

I started this book with one object in mind: I wanted my money back and if I got to fling egg on the faces of those that wronged me then that was an added bonus. I suppose I'd like Top Flight to start jumping again and be what it was. But now, as I enter old age, I want the society I live in to change. I want America to recognize its wrongs, both in the past and currently going on, and then work to right them. I think every black man with drug charges involved in my case . . . should have his case reviewed by a panel of unbiased legal experts.

Epilogue

November 9, 2007

I got up this morning at 9 o'clock like I do every Friday morning. My days are all the same. Gone are the days of teaching, or late-night card games and the intoxicating feeling of running a successful night club. My life has become simple and boring. I do what I have to do and that's it. I have little room in my mind for anything else beyond the rage and feelings of revenge.

I have pretty serious diabetes. It's probably going to kill me. I don't expect to live much longer.

As I write this, the top movie in America is *American Gangster*. I enjoyed this movie but it upset me, throwing into my face the dark feelings that have never really left. One difference between me and Frank Lucas is I've never touched dope and never sold it.

After waking, the first thing I did was call the ABC Board to make the order for Top Flight's whiskey. I read out the various gins and vodkas and whiskeys and all else for my club. The person on the other line reads it back to me and then I hang up. They'll pack up a few crates of bottles for me and then they'll tally the total.

Meanwhile, I go home to exercise. I'm not home a lot. I do forty minutes on my stationary bicycle. I do this every day and it keeps me alive. I don't really like it or not like it. It's just another thing I have to do.

Afterwards, I bathe and shave. I put on a fresh pair of clothes and I walk around the house a little and then I go out to my car. I drive to my club. Montgomery is no better than it was fifteen years ago and in many ways it's a lot worse. The streets look the same. There are a few new businesses, a few boarded up windows where there use to be shops.

I call the ABC Board and ask them how much the whiskey costs. They tell me. I drive to my bank and withdraw the exact amount. The teller doesn't say much and I don't either. I drive to Decatur Street to the ABC Board and I pay in cash. This is my system; I like it and they like it. If the bank likes it I don't know or care. The cases are loaded into my car and I leave. This is every Friday in Richard Thomas's life. This is who I am.

The day was warm but not too hot. I returned to the club and I wrote down on today's receipt how much I spent on the whiskey, vodka, gin, all the booze I sell. My people here help me unload the alcohol. We unpack it into the storage room at Top Flight.

I got all my records together and decided, loosely, what records I'm going to play for happy hour. Today I selected Bobby Blue Bland, the Manhattans, Millie Jackson, and Carl Marshall, among others. I enjoy picking out the music, although I enjoy it less now than I did before. The bulk of the day passes. I spend the time in the upstairs back room, sitting, alone. I did not call my lawyer, I did not call any government people. I did not complain. I sat silent and still in the upstairs room and thought and thought and thought and it amounted to nothing.

I could feel the night beginning to emerge; it was time to get dressed. I like to look good, to wear nice clothes and really do it. This is a function of my personality but also a function of owning a night club. The owner has to look happy, untouchable, unflappable, unmussed. I have to project the fun I want people to have outward. I have to smile and do my best. Therefore, I wear a suit and tie almost all the time. Tonight I put on my black pin-stripe suit.

I emerge from the back room and start playing my records at 5:15. I start with my theme song: "I Need You So" by Ted Taylor. This is my lead song and my customers like it. The music is for them and about them and I spend most of every Friday trying to please them. If I have a bunch of ladies, I hit more records that men sing. If it's half and half, I play sets that they'll both like. I bumped up Carl Marshall's, "Good Loving Will Make You Cry."

About twenty-five people danced, swaying their bodies to the sad songs. Happy hour lasts from 5 until 8:30. I don't drink but I try and appear in spirits. I tell some jokes. There were about a hundred patrons. Before the government and the *Montgomery Advertiser* ruined me, Fridays used to draw 250 to 400. On most nights, you couldn't walk in my club without touching people. Now the reality of a failing night club echoes throughout the empty space.

At 8:30 I got off and went down to my shoe stop. The store was closed. I went into the back room. It's a small room with a couch and a television. And like every Friday night, I thought about how they mistreated me. I just sat there in the back and meditated. It's this consuming feeling, being wronged on such a scale and being helpless to do anything about it. It's turned me angry and bitter. I refuse to let go. I now have hate in my heart and I don't know what to do about it other than stay angry.

I watched *The Godfather*, part 1 on television. It's a great film about a hard man who gets revenge on the people who hurt him and his family. I wondered about my own life while I was watching. I thought about how I could get back, get even, after what they did. I think about everything I can.

I didn't eat. I took a flu shot two weeks ago and its still bothering me. I felt a little sick and the intimations of my own mortality hung over my head. When *The Godfather* ended, I turned the television off and stared out into semi-darkness. These days, I like being alone.

I stayed down there until 2 in the morning. I returned to Top Flight—my work, my life, my refuge, the thing that keeps me busy but also depresses me when I wonder about her former glory—and just thought once more how the forces that be have screwed my life up. I didn't do any cleaning. It had been a slow night so the place was basically clean. The chairs were put on the tables and the air was clear.

I did the cash registers. I checked the money against the sales receipts. And the lights were dimmed then shut off. I walked through my empty club and made sure everything was in its right place. I still felt sick, in my stomach and in my heart.

I walked upstairs to the dressing room in the club and I undressed, I laid down, and I went to sleep. I always sleep well. But I did not dream.

One thought kept running through my head: They screwed me up. They ruined my life. I'd like to say something mean and hateful to Bert Bodiford, to Charles Teschner, but they won't read this book so I won't bother. This is the best thing I can say about either: they're bad people who hurt me and others because they could.

I wish I could end this book on a high note, with a joke, or with some fairytale ending where I got all my money back and everything is back in order. Instead, I have to be frank and clear to face the reality that my life was screwed up by the government. I'm sad, hungry and broke and all the things I worked for in my life, my reputation as a man and as a teacher; my night club and shoe store; my savings that I had worked for since I was a child; relationships with my friends and family—these things were irrevocably destroyed. I then think of my exhausting effort to clear my name and the long, drawn-out process. I constantly recall the investigation performed by Thomas Simon and the written and videoed testimony of Derrick Gaston, an informant who worked for the government for five years. Derrick Gaston stated that the government provided him an apartment in Prattville and financial support in exchange for his testimony against approximately thirty black men; 50 percent of them he never met. When Derrick provided the government with information about a white man selling drugs at a club called The Cave, the agents replied, "With all due respect, Derrick, we only want the niggers." It has become apparent to me that the War on Drugs is a vicious, political front with an ugly, racist agenda. I view it as the anatomy for past, present, and future failure and the perfect blueprint for institutionalized racism. America needs to understand that over 150 lawyers in Montgomery could be indicted for the same reason I was—receiving drug proceeds in the form of payment. After all, when attorneys represent drug dealers, do the dealers go to the bank and borrow $10,000 to pay the retainer or is it drug money? I would conclude that it would be drug proceeds. Therefore, aren't attorneys receiving drug money for payment? These are questions I'd like answered. I'd also like to suggest that we concentrate on the user as much as the dealer simply because we are horribly unsuccessful at curing the drug war by capturing the dealers. Furthermore, there should be drug prevention education taught in preschool. Young children need to see the horrible effects of drugs at an early age and be taught that they are bad for you. It should be part of the curriculum. This would definitely promote drug prevention and character education. Children and adults should be educated about the Drug War and how the courts shouldn't allow convicted felons to testify against others. Also, the United States Attorney's office should choose or appoint members of the court to do the prosecution. Due to how my case was handled, I believe that every man involved in my case should be released. Our founding fathers had great intentions, however they'd never heard of cocaine or marijuana and how the due process of this instance can be manipulated and tainted.

~

NOTES

Notes to Interlude 1

1. Dyer, Joel. *The Perpetual Prisoner Machine*. Boulder: Westview Press, 2000. Page 5.

2. Dyer, page 6.

3. Dyer, page 7.

4. Dyer, page 182.

5. Dyer, page 183.

6. Dyer, page 12.

7. Dyer, page 14.

8. Dyer, page 15.

9. Dyer, page 17.

10. Dyer, page 5.

11. Dyer, page 22.

12. Dyer, page 32.

13. Dyer, page 45.

14. Dyer, page 144.

15. Dyer, page 28.

16. Dyer, page 29.

17. Dyer, page 131.

18. Dyer, page 137.

19. Dyer, page 55.

20. Dyer, page 43.

21. Dyer, page 41.

22. Dyer, page 150.

23. Dyer, page 165.

24. Dyer, page 182.

25. Dyer, page 154.

26. Dyer, page 33.

27. Dyer, page 44.

28. Dyer, page 48.

29. Dyer, page 45.

30. Dyer, page 46.

31. Dyer, page 54.

32. Dyer, page 57.

33. Dyer, page 144.

34. Dyer, page 116.

35. Dyer, page 150.

36. Dyer, page 145.

37. Hervival, Tara, and Paul Wright, eds. *Prison Nation: The Warehousing of America's Poor*. New York: Routledge, 2003. page 19.

38. Hervival, page 27.

39. Ibid.

40. Ibid.

41. Ibid.

42. Dyer, page 28.

Notes to Interlude 2

1. Gray, Mike. *Drug Crazy: How We Got Into This Mess and How We Can Get Out of It*. New York: Random House, 1998. Page 9.

2. Gray, page 178.

3. Dyer, page 183.

4. Gray, page 188.

5. Gray, page 78.

6. Gray, page 74.

7. Gray, page 81.

8. Gray, page 73.

9. Gray, page 75.

10. Ibid.

11. Gray, page 95.

12. Gray, page 101.

13. Gray, page 102.

14. Hervival, page 13.

15. Dyer, page 182.

16. Gray, page 106.

17. Gray, page 151.

18. Gray, page 198.

19. Gray, page 162.

20. Gray, page 191.

21. Gray, page 193.

22. Dyer, page 113.

APPENDIX

We the Senior Class of 1973-74, dedicate our yearbook to

MR. RICHARD Q. THOMAS

for his outstanding teaching of math and the values of life.
We will always remember his good sense of humor
and great personality.

Cloverdale school yearbook dedication, 1974.

Eight appear in court
on cocaine charges

■ **Jail:** One defendant reportedly has 22 children
and may be let out, but the rest will remain in
prison for now

By Tom Hughes
ADVERTISER STAFF WRITER

Eight people accused of taking part in a cocaine conspiracy stretching from Miami to Montgomery appeared before federal magistrates Friday.

As a result, most will remain behind bars until after a federal grand jury considers the charges against them. One defendant — Mary Morrow — reportedly has 22 children and prosecutors will try to work out an arrangement to let her out on bond, said Assistant U.S. Attorney Charles Teschner.

The eight are among 15 defendants who have been charged with conspiring to possess both crack cocaine and cocaine powder with intent to distribute. Investigators contend the conspiracy sold hundreds of kilograms of cocaine and took in millions of dollars under the direction of a Miami man named Oscar Andrews, also known as "The Flower Man."

Mr. Andrews is in custody in Miami and has a detention hearing Tuesday. U.S. Magistrate John Carroll ordered the following defendants held in jail until the grand jury acts:

■ Curtis Drayton, of Central Alabama Auto Brokers on Carter Hill Road. Mr. Drayton was arrested on state cocaine charges in 1989 and later acquitted, but still had to pay $21,600 in taxes under a state law that allows the state to tax dealers for drugs found in their possession.

■ Nathaniel Salery.

■ Don Minnifield.

■ Frank Sowers.

Two defendants had initial appearances before the magistrates Friday, and will have detention hearings Tuesday:

■ Richard "Squirrel" Thomas.

■ Mary Mitchell, wife of Terry Mitchell, another defendant in the case who was arrested last week. Terry Mitchell will have a detention hearing Tuesday.

Two defendants were let out on bond Friday: Ulysses Morris and Dwight Sweeney.

Other defendants in the case who did not appear Friday are:

■ Gerald Wells, who is free on bond.

■ Donald Bozeman, also known as Don Barr, who is free on bond.

■ Robert Lee Franklin, who is being held in jail.

■ Curtis Bell, who has a detention hearing Tuesday.

If convicted, they face from 5 years to life in prison without parole, and possible fines ranging up to $8 million.

Montgomery Advertiser, February 10, 1994.

Narcotics unit chief reports death threats

■ Cocaine ring:
Authorities continue to unravel a tale of interstate trafficking

By Carla Crowder
ADVERTISER STAFF WRITER.

Death threats to Montgomery's head narcotics officer.

Cocaine stashed in dog food bags.

And $300,000 drug hand-offs in small-town Wal-Mart parking lots.

Such are the details beginning to surface as authorities unravel a tale of an interstate cocaine-trafficking ring whose tentacles reach to local crack dealers.

At least 16 suspects have been implicated, millions of dollars seized and hundreds of pounds of cocaine sold during the 2½-year probe. Authorities say Miami man Oscar Andrews is the ring leader of a network of central Alabama cohorts.

Hearings were held Monday to determine whether Mr. Andrews and five others should remain behind bars until trial.

Federal Magistrate Judge John Carroll, who presided over the hearings, called the operation a "serious, very serious drug distribution ring, the most serious I've seen in my seven years on the bench."

The bust of the multitiered organization should temporarily drain Montgomery's cocaine supply to street-level crack dealers, authorities say.

Even after the arrests, danger exists for witnesses and law enforcement officers, according to the testimony of Maj. Larry Armstead, who heads the Montgomery Police Department's

Please turn to **THREATS, 4A**

THREATS

from page 1A

narcotics unit.

On Friday, "a gentleman came to my office, and I was advised that I was messing with the wrong people, to watch my back and that these people were not kidding, were not playing," said Maj. Armstead.

A day later, he noticed someone watching him from a white car as he was leaving a local mall. The car then trailed him down East South Boulevard to Interstate 85, Maj. Armstead said.

The white car nipped at his bumper at speeds up to 95 mph before Maj. Armstead spotted a state trooper and asked him to stop the white car. Once stopped, the driver shouted the name "Armstrong" at Maj. Armstead, denied following him and told conflicting stories about why he was speeding.

Officers discovered the driver, who was charged with DUI, was from the south Alabama town of Castleberry — one of four pivotal locations for the shattered drug ring.

As a result of Monday's hearings:

■ Mr. Andrews, whose hearing was held in Miami, will be jailed until trial. Federal authorities plan to send him to Montgomery as soon as possible, said executive U.S. attorney Don Rasher.

■ Terry Mitchell, of Castleberry, will be detained without bond until trial.

Drug Enforcement Agent Jack Wall testified that authorities witnessed Mr. Mitchell exchange cocaine for cash twice in a Greenville Wal-Mart parking lot.

After a Jan. 30 exchange, he delivered drugs to accused co-conspirator Curtis Drayton at a Carter Hill Road car lot, where 3 kilograms of cocaine were transferred to a dog food bag. Officers later stopped Mr. Drayton and seized the drugs from his car.

The cocaine carries a street value of $300,000, Mr. Wall said.

A portly man wearing bright-orange jail coveralls, Mr. Mitchell waved and smiled while being led away.

■ Mary Mitchell, a Miami hair stylist, has been married to Mr. Mitchell 24 years and often returns to Castleberry. Authorities have a tape-recording of a telephone conversation between the couple in which she checks on a drug deal, Mr. Wall said.

Judge Carroll ordered Mrs. Mitchell released until trial under "rigid conditions of where she goes and whom she sees."

■ Curtis Bell, who authorities say controlled communications in Montgomery for Mr. Andrews, remains detained. His hearing was postponed because he did not have an attorney.

■ Lorenzo "Lo Lo" Hughes, who operated out of a Vaughn Lakes apartment, will be jailed until trial. "The evidence is clear that Mr. Hughes is a major drug distributor in this area and with that comes the presumption of danger to witnesses and to law enforcement," Judge Carroll said.

■ Richard "Squirrel" Thomas, owner of Top Flight Disco, was released on $100,000 property bond secured by his house and ordered to stay away from his nightclub during business hours.

Mr. Thomas is accused of laundering money for the cocaine traffickers, Mr. Wall said.

A grand jury meets today in the case. It's expected to report back Thursday.

Montgomery Advertiser, **February 23, 1994.**

Authorities net 19 arrests in fishy cocaine ring

■ Miami connection: Most of the suspects in the conspiracy are from Montgomery, officials say

By Carla Crowder
ADVERTISER STAFF WRITER

A seafood shipment arrived at Dannelly Field from Miami. Geraldine Frazier picked up the fish as she had other Miami fish shipments, authorities say. And like other shipments, these fish were

stuffed with cocaine.

Law enforcement agents say they were watching Jan. 31 when Mrs. Frazier gathered her fish and drove away from the airport.

She was arrested shortly after — one of 19 people authorities say is involved in a cocaine conspiracy controlled by Oscar

came to a close about 10 days ago, when they rounded up suspects, mostly in Montgomery.

A federal grand jury has been

meeting since Thursday on the case.

According to federal court records, Mr. Andrews controlled the cocaine. A network of couriers, dealers and money launderers within the multitiered organization distributed hundreds of pounds of it. Profits reached

"Flower Man" Andrews.

Hoping to dissolve the ring, authorities in September 1992 formed a task force. The probe

millions of dollars.

Mr. Andrews' cohorts include a former junior high mathematics teacher, a Plantersville grandmother on welfare and a downtown Montgomery body-shop owner, court documents state.

Mrs. Frazier, who picked up

Please turn to **ARRESTS, 6A**

ARRESTS

from page 1A

the fish, is the mother of Mr. Andrews' school-age son, court records state.

During the 2½-year investigation, agents used phone taps, videotapes of drug sales and dozens of informants to make their case. In all, 18 of 19 suspects have been arrested.

Miami connections

Drug Enforcement Agent Jack Wall called Mr. Andrews "a career criminal."

From Miami, Mr. Andrews shipped cocaine to warehouses, one in the tiny Autauga County town of Plantersville and another in Castleberry, a south Alabama community, Agent Wall testified. Until early 1993, Mr. Andrews used a third warehouse, called "the compound," at 11487 Atlanta Highway in far east Montgomery, court records state.

These warehouses were controlled by:
■ Curtis Bell, a longtime asso-

10-kilogram amounts to the next level in the organization, investigators said. A kilogram is about 2.2 pounds.

These people, called lieutenants, sold cocaine to street dealers. According to court records, lieutenants arrested are:

■ Curtis Drayton, 37, who dealt cocaine out of Central Alabama Auto Brokers, 1455 Carter Hill Road. When police began cracking down, Mr. Drayton was one of the first stopped. Police seized 3 kilograms, about 6.6 pounds, of cocaine from him after a Jan. 30 traffic stop. He told Mr. Mitchell and Mr. Andrews that he'd been "ripped off by police," court records state. Mr. Andrews didn't believe him and ordered him to pay $75,000, court records state.

Mr. Drayton was indicted on cocaine-trafficking charges in 1990, but a judge found him not guilty, according to Montgomery County Circuit Court records.

■ Nathaniel Salery, 32, a felon who has been on probation but has never served time for shooting into a vehicle and theft convictions, according to circuit court records. He operated out of

Cocaine ring

A two-year cocaine investigation by federal, state and local authorities ended last week with a string of arrests. Investigators listed the following suspects along with the roles they are accused of playing in the interstate cocaine ring:

Ring leader:
■ Oscar "Flower Man" Andrews of Miami, formerly of Montgomery.

Distribution chiefs:
■ Curtis Bell — controlled Montgomery operations, managed communications center and cocaine warehouse on Atlanta Highway.
■ Mary Morrow — stored cocaine in her Plantersville home.
■ Terry Mitchell — from his Castleberry residence distributed cocaine to Montgomery traffickers and took profits to Mr. Andrews. Mr. Mitchell's wife, Mary, of Miami also is implicated.

Money launderer:
✗■ Richard "Squirrel" Thomas — owner of Top Flight Disco, helped facilitate drug transactions by money laundering.

Lieutenants:

Miami connections

Drug Enforcement Agent Jack Wall called Mr. Andrews "a career criminal."

From Miami, Mr. Andrews shipped cocaine to warehouses, one in the tiny Autauga County town of Plantersville and another in Castleberry, a south Alabama community, Agent Wall testified. Until early 1993, Mr. Andrews used a third warehouse, called "the compound," at 11487 Atlanta Highway in far east Montgomery, court records state.

These warehouses were controlled by:

■ Curtis Bell, a longtime associate of Mr. Andrews, who managed the Atlanta Highway compound. Curtis Bell served as a person to relay messages, deliver money, and from time to time, deliver cocaine," according to an affidavit by DEA Agent Marshall Simons.

Mr. Bell was arrested Feb. 16 and remained behind bars Thursday.

■ Terry Wayne Mitchell, a part-time roofer who managed the Castleberry warehouse.

Mr. Mitchell "travels to Miami to deposit cash derived from cocaine sales. When he returns from Miami, he brings multi-kilogram quantities of cocaine," according to Agent Simons' affidavit.

On Jan. 28, Mr. Mitchell returned from Miami pulling a U-Haul trailer. On Feb. 15, after another of his Miami trips, agents searched Mr. Mitchell's pickup and seized more than 28 pounds of cocaine, records state.

A federal judge ordered Mr. Mitchell behind bars until trial.

■ Mary Mitchell, wife of Mr. Mitchell, is a hair stylist who lives in Miami. Together, she and Mr. Mitchell maintain a home in Castleberry and one in Miami on a combined income of about $1,800 a month, according to forms they signed to apply for court-appointed attorneys.

Mrs. Mitchell was released until trial.

■ Mary E. Morrow, a mother of 22 children and a grandmother, oversaw the Plantersville warehouse. She "receives deliveries of cocaine from Mr. Mitchell and delivers cocaine to cocaine dealers in Montgomery, Birmingham and Clanton," according to Mr. Simons' affidavit.

After Mr. Andrews shipped cocaine to these warehouses, the managers distributed it in 1- to

seized 3 kilograms, about 6.6 pounds, of cocaine from him after a Jan. 30 traffic stop. He told Mr. Mitchell and Mr. Andrews that he'd been "ripped off by police," court records state. Mr. Andrews didn't believe him and ordered him to pay $75,000, court records state.

Mr. Drayton was indicted on cocaine-trafficking charges in 1990, but a judge found him not guilty, according to Montgomery County Circuit Court records.

■ Nathaniel Salery, 32, a felon who has been on probation but has never served time for shooting into a vehicle and theft convictions, according to circuit court records. He operated out of a Woodley Park house, court records state.

■ Lorenzo "Lo Lo" Hughes. He appears three times in videotapes selling cocaine. Both he and Mr. Salery remain behind bars until trial.

■ Robert Lee Franklin. He received shipments from Mr. Bell and Mr. Mitchell, including one in December 1993 in which he paid $25,000 for a kilogram of cocaine, court records state.

Others Implicated

Following is a list of others arrested in the case, according to court records:

✗■ Richard "Squirrel" Thomas, former math teacher at Cloverdale Junior High School, who now owns Top Flight Disco. Mr. Thomas is accused of placing bets for Mr. Andrews and using a gambling scheme to launder drug money. He has been released on $100,000 bond.

■ Don Minefield, 35, known as "Billy Al," used his business, Pop's Paint and Body, 534 N. Lawrence St., to "sell, store and conceal drugs and drug proceeds," according to a federal court affidavit from ABC Agent J.M. Whitaker.

■ Donald James Bozeman, 46, owns Don Bar Appliance and Air Conditioning. Authorities say he dealt 5 to 6 ounces of cocaine each week through his business and several east Montgomery nightclubs. A married man and father, Mr. Bozeman lives in a $70,000 house in Wetumpka.

■ Jerry Wells, 48, 184 S. Burbank Drive, is accused of dealing cocaine from his nightclub, the Diplomat Lounge on Norman Bridge Road. The lounge is now under new ownership. Mr. Wells has been released until trial on

$50,000 bond, court records state.

■ Frank Sowers, 34, often sold cocaine to Mr. Bozeman, authorities say.

■ Ronald "Squiggy" Lander, 29, sold cocaine out of a south Montgomery home, according to a police report.

■ Ulysses Morris, 31, lent money to Mr. Drayton to pay Mr. Flowers for cocaine, court records state.

■ Dwight Sweeney, 19, and Lloyd McDaniel sold $6,000 in cocaine to an informant Jan. 24, court records state. Both carried 9mm handguns when they were arrested.

Club owner's drug charges withdrawn

■ Mystery: Attorneys refused to detail why Richard 'Squirrel' Thomas, is now cleared

By Carla Crowder
ADVERTISER STAFF WRITER

Prosecutors have dropped drug charges against nightclub owner and former math teacher Richard "Squirrel" Thomas, initially implicated in a massive Miami-to-Montgomery cocaine ring.

Mr. Thomas' name does not appear in a new indictment filed earlier this week, which supercedes two previous federal court indictments.

Government attorneys refused to detail why a man they'd accused of being the money-launderer and a major player for the drug ring is now cleared.

"He's no longer part of it," said Assistant U.S. Attorney Don Rasher, declining further comment.

Mr. Thomas, who owns Top Flight Disco on High Street and is a retired math teacher from Cloverdale Junior High School, was indicted in February on charges of possession with intent to distribute cocaine and cocaine base.

More specifically, the original indictment states that Mr. Thomas in December 1993, accepted $25,000 in drug proceeds from Oscar "Flower Man" Andrews' in payment of a gambling debt.

Authorities say Andrews was kingpin of the multi-million dollar ring.

Also, the original indictment states that Mr. Thomas on Jan. 30, 1994, possessed more than five kilograms of cocaine and Feb. 17 carried two semiautomatic handguns while committing drug crimes.

A motion filed Wednesday by defense attorneys alleges that Mr. Thomas has agreed to testify against Curtis Drayton and Curtis Bell, two men accused of transporting and distributing millions of dollars in cocaine for the ring.

When asked why the charges against his client were dropped, Mr. Thomas' attorney, Euel Screws Jr., said he couldn't comment except to say that "It's not a deal, so to speak."

Mr. Rasher pointed out that "the superceding indictment brought in a new party and eliminated him."

The new indictment adds Jerry Lindsey Artis to the list of 17 defendants.

Mr. Artis, who owns a house in

Please turn to **CHARGES, 2B**

Montgomery Advertiser, June 10, 1994 (Continued on next page).

CHARGES

from page 1B

Center Point, a town just north of Birmingham, bought and sold 12 to 20 kilograms of cocaine a month during 1990 and 1991 and possibly longer, according to court records.

Mr. Thomas could not be reached for comment. His attorney, Mr. Screws, issued a response on his behalf that states, "We believe that the United States Attorney realized, after careful examination of all the evidence, that Richard Thomas was not involved in any drug conspiracy, nor was he guilty of distributing, possession, selling or handling drugs or controlled substances."

Authorities say the Andrews drug ring was responsible for half the cocaine and crack cocaine shipped into Montgomery. Mr. Andrews, who lives in Miami, and others were indicted in February after a multiagency drug bust.

The case is scheduled for trial in early August.

APPENDIX

At approximately 10:30 AM on 12-28-92, I met with Mr. Simmons and a few other agents at the DEA office. We then beeped Curtis from my car phone and he promptly returned the call which we then recorded. We agreed to meet at his office at 12:00 PM to make the exchange. We all then proceeded after I was searched along with my car to a parking lot where the recording device was activated. I arrived at his office at 12:10 PM and waited for Curtis to arrive. Upon his arrival, I exchanged $1,000 for 1 ounce of Cocaine. The agents and I then returned to the office and I was searched again along with my car. I gave the cocaine received from Curtis to Marshall Simmons.

I beeped him again and made sure he was ready to make the exchange. He told me to meet him at his office and he would be there shortly.

I have read the foregoing statement and it is true and correct to the best of my knowledge and belief. I have given this statement freely and voluntarily, without threats, coercion, or promises.

Chappell Hill
12-28-92

W. Marshall Simmons 12/28/92

D. W. _____ 12-28

Affidavit of Chappell Hill, December 28, 1992.

statement of MPD LI # N-144 at approximately 3:30pm on 1/8/93, given to S/A Simmons and MPD Det. Roy regarding the purchase of Ex & off one ounce of cocaine) from Curtis Drayton on 1/8/93 in 60-93 7001.

1-8-93

At approximately 1.43 PM on 1-8-93, I beeped CURTIS DRAYTON and he returned my call shortly thereafter on my carphone. At this time, we agr for me to call him again at 3.30 PM to make arrangements to meet. I then phoned him again at 3.00 PM and agreed to meet ASAP at his office. I was then searched and fitted with a ~~transmitter~~ device and my car was sear. Marshall Simmons and two agents then proceede with me to the location. Upon arriving at Con Alabama Auto Brokers, Curtis entered my car and instructed me to go to Dave's Watch shop w him. On the way there, he gave me some c Cocaine in exchange for $1,000.⁰⁰ provided to m by the DEA. We then returned to the car lot and I returned to the office (DEA) and hande over the Cocaine. My car was then searched again as well as my person.

Chappell Hill
1-8-93
By Marshall Simmons 1/8

#5

Affidavit of Chappell Hill, April 8, 1993.

1   All right. You may stand down.

2   Call your next witness.

3   MR. TESCHNER: The United States next calls

4 Chappell Hill.

5   MR. GLASSROTH: I want to get those exhibits

6 straight and tender those in a moment, Your Honor.

7   THE COURT: All right.

8   MR. GLASSROTH: If I may check with the clerk?

9   THE COURT: Sure.

10   THE CLERK: Come around to the witness stand and be

11 seated.

12   MR. GLASSROTH: Your Honor, at this time I would

13 like to offer into evidence Defendant Wallace Salery's

14 Exhibits Numbers 1, 3, 4, and 5.

15   MR. TESCHNER: No objection, Your Honor.

16   THE COURT: All right. They are admitted.

17   (Defendant Wallace Salery's Exhibits Number 1, Number 3,

18 Number 4, and Number 5 received in evidence)

19   CHAPPELL HILL, GOVERNMENT'S WITNESS, PREVIOUSLY SWORN

20   THE CLERK: You have been sworn, haven't you?

21   THE WITNESS: Yes, sir.

22   THE CLERK: Please state your full name, spell your

23 last, state your residence and occupation.

24   THE WITNESS: My full name is Chappell Henry

25 Lipston Hill. The last name is spelled H-I-L-L. And I

Chappell Hill testimony transcript, page 68.

1   reside in Jefferson County.

2   DIRECT EXAMINATION

3   BY MR. TESCHNER:

4   Q. Mr. Hill could you please lean forward a little bit so

5   you can be picked up by the microphones.

6   Sir, I want to take your attention back to the month of

7   November/December time frame of 1992.

8   Could you tell the jury what you were doing at that

9   time?

10 A. I was attending schooling in Tuscaloosa.

11 Q. And what school were you attending?

12 A. University of Alabama.

13 Q. What were your studies there?

14 A. Business.

15 Q. And what degree were you pursing?

16 A. My master's.

17 Q. Sir, at the time around Thanksgiving, between

18 Thanksgiving and Christmas, were you confronted by

19 authorities at the campus there?

20 A. Yes, I was.

21 Q. Could you tell the jury what happened or why you were

22 confronted by authorities?

23 A. I was -- a confidential informant rolled over on me, and

24 that's why I was confronted. He had taken three grams of

25 cocaine from my apartment -- approximately.

Chappell Hill testimony transcript, page 69.

1   Q. I'm sorry? Three grams of cocaine?

2   A. Approximately three grams. I'm not exactly sure of the

3   exact amount.

4   Q. At the time that -- at that time that you were notified

5   of that, were you placed under arrest?

6   A. No, I was not.

7   Q. Did the police officers indicate to you that they had

8   evidence of your involvement in that cocaine transaction?

9   A. That's correct.

10 Q. Could you tell the jury whether or not you reached an

11 agreement with those police officers?

12 A. I was instructed either to talk with them then or to

13 contact an attorney. And I opted to contact an attorney.

14 Q. After you contacted an attorney, what did you do?

15 A. I had the option of trying to fight it or to cooperate.

16 And my attorney advised me to cooperate.

17 Q. Now when you agreed on the advice of your attorney to

18 cooperate, what sort of agreement did you reach with the

19 police?

20 A. That I would make three buys.

21 Q. Could you tell the jury who you agreed to make buys

22 from?

23 A. Curtis Drayton.

24 Q. Could you tell the jury why it was that you agreed to

25 make buys from Mr. Drayton?

Chappell Hill testimony transcript, page 70.

1   A. That's the only person I had ever bought from.

2   Q. And what had you bought from Mr. Drayton previously?

3   A. I had bought a total of two ounces of cocaine.

4   Q. Now after you entered into the agreement to cooperate,

5   did you work with authorities here in Montgomery?

6   A. That's correct.

7   Q. Could you tell the jury who you worked with?

8   A. I worked with Marshall Simons and a Detective Roy and

9   Cathy and Mark Whitaker.

10 Q. And do you recall the date of the 18th of December of

11 1992?

12 A. I do.

13 Q. Could you tell the jury what happened on that day?

14 A. I was instructed to meet at the DEA Office. And at that

15 time I was instructed to page Curtis and set up a time for a

16 buy.

17 Q. Were you successful in doing that?

18 A. That's correct.

19 Q. What did the agents do to prepare you to go make that

20 buy?

21 A. They fitted me with a wiring device and gave me the

22 instructions on what to do and then followed me to the

23 location.

24 Q. Did they provide you with anything in the way of money

25 to make the buy?

Chappell Hill testimony transcript, page 71.

1 A. Right, one thousand.

2 Q. Could you tell the jury how much they gave you?

3 A. One thousand dollars.

4 Q. And after -- were you searched?

5 A. Yes, I was.

6 Q. And was your car searched?

7 A. Yes, it was searched.

8 Q. And where did you go to make your purchase?

9 A. To the car lot, which was Central Alabama Auto Brokers.

10 Q. Could you tell the jury the location of Central Alabama

11 Auto Brokers?

12 A. It's on Carter Hill Road near Forest Avenue school.

13 Q. Now what happened when you went down to the car lot?

14 A. I met with Curtis. And I believe we got into my car and

15 drove around the block and then returned.

16   And then I returned to the DEA Office.

17 Q. Could you tell the jury what happened in the ride around

18 the block?

19 A. That's when we made the transaction.

20 Q. After you got back to the car lot, what happened?

21 A. After I got back to the car lot?

22 Q. Yes.

23 A. He got out of the car. And then I went back to the DEA

24 Office.

25 Q. When you got back to the DEA Office, what did you do?

Chappell Hill testimony transcript, page 72.

1   A. I turned over the evidence and wrote a statement. And

2   that was it.

3   And I agreed on another time to make another buy in the

4   future.

5   Q. Were you searched at the time you turned over the

6   evidence?

7   A. Right.

8   Q. And was your car searched?

9   A. Right, it was.

10   Q. Now do you recall what the next date was when you made a

11   purchase?

12   A. It was the 28th of December.

13   Q. And what happened on that day?

14   A. Basically, the same scenario. I went to the DEA Office.

15   We set up a time. I set up a time with Curtis when I was

16   going to meet him.

17   I went to the car lot. We didn't ever leave that time.

18   We made the exchange, and then I returned to the DEA Office

19   and went through the same scenario.

20   Q. And what did you purchase that day?

21   A. The same, one ounce of cocaine for a thousand dollars.

22   Q. Did you have another occasion to make a buy?

23   A. One more.

24   Q. Could you tell the jury what when that was?

25   A. January 8th.

Chappell Hill testimony transcript, page 73.

1 Q. Of 1993?

2 A. Correct.

3 Q. And what happened on that day?

4 A. I went to the DEA Office, set up a time to meet over the

5 phone with Curtis, went to the car lot and picked him up.

6 And we left and made the transaction.

7   And then I returned and went back to the DEA Office.

8 Q. And how much did you purchase on that occasion?

9 A. One ounce of cocaine for one thousand dollars.

10 Q. Mr. Hill, as a result of your cooperation, were you --

11 you were never formally charged with any violation; is that

12 correct?

13 A. That's correct.

14 Q. And were you able to graduate from college?

15 A. That's correct.

16   MR. TESCHNER: I have no further questions, Your

17 Honor.

18   THE COURT: All right, Mr. Wise.

19   CROSS EXAMINATION

20 BY MR. WISE:

21 Q. Mr. Hill, did you testify that you were working on your

22 master's degree or you had received it?

23 A. I was working on it at the time, and I did receive it.

24 Q. Where are you working?

25 A. In Birmingham.

Chappell Hill testimony transcript, page 74.

1   Q. Where?

2   A. I am working with an investment firm.

3   Q. How long have you been working with them?

4   A. About fourteen months.

5   Q. And you testified that in 1992 in Tuscaloosa -- and I

6   didn't hear exactly what you said -- something about three

7   grams of cocaine. What was that?

8   A. There was three grams that I agreed to buy in the

9   future, and I had bought two prior to that.

10   Q. Well, you were talking about the police coming to you.

11   Did they find cocaine on you in Tuscaloosa?

12   A. They had sent someone in that came into my apartment and

13   got it. And he was wired. And then he left. And then

14   about thirty minutes later, they came in.

15   Q. Did someone come to your apartment and buy cocaine?

16   A. Well, he didn't actually buy. He was -- he came in my

17   apartment, and he was going to pay me back later for it.

18   And he took it and was going to sell it.

19   Q. How much cocaine did you have that day when he came in

20   your apartment wired?

21   A. Well, there was a portion of an ounce of cocaine, which

22   was the second ounce that I had bought.

23   Q. How much cocaine did he leave with that day?

24   A. I'm not sure how much he left with because he went back

25   and got it out of my closet.

Chappell Hill testimony transcript, page 75.

1   Q. Did he know --

2   A. So I don't know how much he left with the first time he

3   left.

4   Q. Did he know where you kept it?

5   A. Yes, he did.

6   Q. Had he been over to your apartment before and observed

7   cocaine in your possession?

8   A. That's correct.

9   Q. And you all had done cocaine together?

10 A. No, we had not done cocaine together.

11 Q. Had you given him or sold him cocaine before?

12 A. Well, he was actually selling the cocaine to other

13 people. And he was getting it from me, and then he would

14 just pay me, you know, when he was through selling it.

15   Like I said, we had only done it twice, so it wasn't

16 like there was a system or particular way of doing it.

17 Q. So he was selling cocaine for you?

18 A. Correct.

19 Q. And when you say that he went back to your closet, did

20 you have it hidden in your closet?

21 A. It was in one of my drawers in my dresser.

22 Q. I'm sorry, sir. I didn't hear you.

23 A. In the dresser drawer.

24 Q. In the drawer itself?

25 A. Right.

Chappell Hill testimony transcript, page 76.

1   Q. Was it hidden up underneath some socks or something?

2   A. It was in my sock drawer, but it -- I mean -- it was

3   visible when you opened the drawer.

4   Q. You just had it sitting on top of your socks?

5   A. Correct.

6   Q. Did you live by yourself in Tuscaloosa?A. No, I did

7   not.

8   Q. Was this fellow who was selling cocaine for you, was he

9   your roommate?

10   A. No, he was not.

11   Q. Was your roommate involved in selling cocaine with you?

12   A. No, he was not.

13   Q. Was he aware that you were selling cocaine?

14   A. He was aware.

15   Q. Was he aware of where you kept your cocaine?

16   A. I don't -- I'm not sure.

17   Q. Did you always keep it in the sock drawer?

18   A. I had only, like I said, done it twice. So the other

19   two times, yes, I had.

20   Q. And this fellow that went back in the back with your

21   permission to get the cocaine out of your sock drawer to

22   sell it, you did not get any money from him at that time?

23   A. Correct.

24   Q. And you can't tell us how much cocaine he left with.

25   A. It was less than an ounce. That's all I can tell you

Chappell Hill testimony transcript, page 77.

1   because I'm not sure how much he had gotten prior to that.

2   I just know he was going to pay me in full when he had

3   collected for the full ounce.

4   Q. And how much would an ounce sell for, Mr. Hill?

5   A. There's sixteen grams in an ounce, and I think he was

6   selling them for ninety dollars a gram.

7   Q. And you can't tell us how much cocaine was left in your

8   sock drawer after he took out what he was going to sell?

9   A. When he came back, I know he had -- the last -- when he

10 came back and he was wired, he got three grams, if I'm not

11 mistaken.

12   So I would say it was somewhere between one and thirteen

13 grams.

14 Q. And you were never arrested?

15 A. No, I was not. But I was told I would be arrested, but

16 I needed to talk to my lawyer first. And if I didn't agree

17 to cooperate, I would be arrested.

18 Q. And you talked to your lawyer?

19 A. Right.

20 Q. Who was your lawyer?

21 A. It was -- he is with Prince, Bared and Poole.

22 Q. Up in Tuscaloosa?

23 A. Right.

24 Q. And it was then that you decided that having got caught

25 dealing drugs, you were going to what is called cooperate;

Chappell Hill testimony transcript, page 78.

1 is that correct? Sir?

2 A. Correct.

3 Q. And not only were you not convicted of this offense, but

4 your dealing was they weren't even going to charge you for

5 it.

6 A. That's correct.

7 Q. And right now there is no record of arrest on you, is

8 there, indicating that you were charged --

9 A. That's correct.

10 Q. -- with any cocaine violation whatsoever?

11 A. That's correct.

12 Q. Pretty good deal, Mr. Hill, isn't it?

13 A. It was.

14 Q. And you knew that at the time, didn't you?

15 A. I did.

16 Q. And your lawyer told you that, didn't he?

17 A. He did.

18 Q. And lawyer, did he also not tell you that normally

19 you're going to be arrested and have to plead to something?

20 A. If I didn't cooperate, he said that would happen.

21 Q. Did he also tell you though that not even having an

22 arrest record and cutting a deal like that was

23 extraordinary?

24 A. I don't recall if he said it was an extraordinary

25 situation, but he did say it was a good deal.

Chappell Hill testimony transcript, page 79.

1   Q. All right. And you understood that, didn't you?

2   A. I did.

3   Q. And you felt like this was a great program you were

4   fixing to get on, didn't you?

5   A. I felt like it was a good deal considering the

6   circumstances.

7   Q. It was a good deal for you, correct, Mr. Hill?

8   A. Correct.

9   Q. Now you testified that you agreed to make three buys; is

10 that correct?

11 A. That's correct.

12 Q. With whom did you make this agreement?

13 A. With Marshall Simons -- you mean with whom did I --

14 Q. With what law enforcement officials did you agree to

15 make three buys so that you wouldn't even have an arrest

16 record?

17 A. My lawyer set it up with the office here. And Marshall

18 Simons was who they set it up with.

19 Q. So it was all done in Montgomery.

20 A. The agreement was actually done out at Tuscaloosa

21 because my lawyer was in Tuscaloosa. He set the agreement

22 up with them in Montgomery.

23 Q. And this is Marshall Simons sitting right here, correct?

24 A. That is correct.

25 Q. Who else was involved besides Marshall Simons with law

Chappell Hill testimony transcript, page 80.

1   enforcement?

2   A.   Cathy was.

3   Q.   Cathy Watts?

4   A.   And Mark Whitaker.

5   Q.   Mark Whitaker?

6   A.   Right.

7   Q.   All right.   And did you sign a written agreement?

8   A.   I don't recall.

9   MR. WISE: Your Honor, if there was a written

10 agreement, we would ask that it be produced.

11   MR. TESCHNER: I'm not aware of any written

12 agreement, Your Honor.

13   MR. WISE: Fine.

14 BY MR. WISE:

15 Q.   So not only were you not going to have an arrest, but

16 you had an agreement based on a handshake, correct?

17 A.   An agreement based on what my lawyer had worked out.

18 That is correct.

19 Q.   But there was no written agreement to your knowledge

20 that you signed?

21 A.   Not to my knowledge, correct.

22 Q.   And they told you, did they not, that they wanted you to

23 buy cocaine from Curtis Drayton?

24 A.   That is correct.

25 Q.   That was their wish, correct?

Chappell Hill testimony transcript, page 81.

1   A.   That was -- yes, that's who I agreed to buy from.

2   Q.   All right. And how old were you in 1992 -- December of

3   '92?

4   A.   I was twenty three.

5   Q.   Twenty-three. How old are you now?

6   A.   Twenty-five.

7   Q.   You testified that on December 18, 1992, that you were

8   given instructions as to what to do.

9   A.   Correct.

10 Q.   What were those instructions?

11 A.   To set up a time to meet to make the exchange. And I

12 was fitted with a wiring device, as I said earlier, and

13 instructed to go make the exchange and to return following

14 the exchange.

15 Q.   Were any instructions given to you by any law

16 enforcement officials as to what they wanted you to say on

17 the tape or what they would like for Curtis Drayton to say

18 on the tape?

19 A.   No, no instructions were given of that nature.

20 Q.   No one told you they wanted to get you to get Curtis

21 Drayton to talk about drugs on the tape?

22 A.   No one told me.

23 Q.   Sir?

24 A.   No one told me that.

25 Q.   Tell me about the search of your automobile.

Chappell Hill testimony transcript, page 82.

1   What kind of car did you have?

2   A.   I had an Acura.

3   Q.   Tell me about the search of the automobile prior to

4   going to Central Alabama Auto Brokers.

5   A.   I don't know what that consisted of. I was in the

6   office when my car was searched.

7   Q.   How long did it take to search your car?

8   A.   I'm not sure how long that took.

9   Q.   Tell us about the search of your person. What were you

10   wearing that day?

11   A.   A button-down shirt and either blue jeans or a pair of

12   khakis.

13   Q.   Who searched you?

14   A.   I don't recall.

15   Q.   Tell us about the search.

16   A.   It was just a normal -- they checked your ankles, legs.

17   Q.   How did they check them?

18   A.   Just felt them.

19   Q.   Did they take your socks off?

20   A.   No, they did not.

21   Q.   Did they take your shoes off?

22   A.   I don't recall.

23   Q.   Did they check to see what you had in your sock

24   underneath your foot?

25   A.   I don't believe they did.

Chappell Hill testimony transcript, page 83.

1   Q. It was just a pat-down type search?

2   A. If I'm not mistaken. But I don't recall the search

3   thoroughly, but I think I would remember if they had taken

4   my socks off.

5   Q. Did anyone stick their hands in your pockets?

6   A. Yes, they did.

7   Q. Did anyone ask you to take your pants off?

8   A. No, they did not.

9   Q. Did you take any clothing off at all dealing with this

10   so-called search?

11   A. I unbuttoned my button-down shirt.

12   Q. How many buttons did you have on your shirt?

13   A. Six or seven.

14   Q. Was it all the way down the front?

15   A. Right.

16   Q. But you did not remove your socks to your knowledge,

17   your shoes to your knowledge or your pants to your

18   knowledge?

19   A. That's correct.

20   Q. Correct?

21   A. Correct.

22   Q. Did anyone check to see if you had anything in your

23   underwear?

24   A. No, they did not.

25   Q. And that would be true for all three occasions we're

Chappell Hill testimony transcript, page 84.

1   talking about here today, is it not, Mr. Hill?

2   A. That's correct.

3   Q. On the second occasion, did anyone search your car in

4   your presence?

5   A. No, they did not.

6   Q. On the third occasion, did they search your car in your

7   presence?

8   A. No, they did not. I believe I was in the office on all

9   three objections.

10   Q. And the searches of your body were the same on all three

11   occasions; were they not?

12   A. That's correct.

13   Q. And they were done by whom, Mr. Simons?

14   A. I don't recall who did the actual search of my body. I

15   would think it was probably Marshall.

16   Q. Let's talk about the first day, December 18, '92,

17   correct?

18   A. Correct.

19   Q. You testified that you pulled up to Central Alabama Auto

20   Brokers and that Mr. Drayton got in the vehicle with you,

21   correct?

22   A. That's correct.

23   Q. Where did you all drive?

24   A. I believe we drove around near Forest Avenue school.

25   Q. Were you followed by Mr. Simons to your knowledge?

Chappell Hill testimony transcript, page 85.

1   A. I was told that they were watching, but, I mean, I

2   wasn't watching in my rear view mirror.

3   Q. Okay. How long were you and Mr. Drayton gone in your

4   vehicle?

5   A. Very briefly.

6   Q. And have you seen the transcript -- you had on a body

7   wire, correct?

8   A. Yes, I have seen that.

9   Q. You had on a body wire, correct?

10 A. Right.

11 Q. On all three occasions?

12 A. Correct.

13 Q. And have you seen a transcript that was done of that

14 body wire of the conversation that you and Mr. Drayton had

15 in the automobile that day on December 18, '92?

16 A. I have.

17 Q. And not one word was mentioned in that conversation when

18 he was in the car that day that dealt with drugs, true?

19 A. That's correct.

20 Q. He never mentioned drugs, did he?

21 A. That's correct.

22 Q. You never mentioned drugs, did you?

23 A. That's correct.

24 Q. No one mentioned money.

25 A. That's correct.

Chappell Hill testimony transcript, page 86.

1   Q. You didn't and he didn't?

2   A. That's correct.

3   Q. In fact, it is a casual conversation; is it not?

4   A. That's correct.

5   Q. Dealing with his car business, some cars he had on the

6   lot, their condition, and what he hopes to get for them,

7   correct?

8   A. I believe that's correct.

9   Q. All right. Now let's go to December 28th, '92.

10   A. Okay.

11   Q. You have already testified you didn't see the search of

12   your automobile, correct?

13   A. Correct.

14   Q. The search of your person was basically the same as the

15   first time, correct?

16   A. That's correct.

17   Q. And you, once again, when over and picked up Curtis

18   Drayton and he got in your automobile, correct?

19   A. That is correct.

20   Q. Where did you all go?

21   A. The second time we actually never left the business, if

22   I'm not mistaken. I walked in the business and stayed in

23   there for a relatively short period of time.

24   And then I returned to the DEA Office.

25   Q. All right. And once again, you had on a body mike,

Chappell Hill testimony transcript, page 87.

1 correct?

2 A. That's correct.

3 Q. And have you reviewed the transcript of the body mike

4 recording that was done dealing with January the 8th, 1993?

5 A. Yes, I have.

6 Q. And once again, there is no mention by Curtis Drayton

7 nor yourself about drugs, correct?

8 A. Correct.

9 Q. No mention by Curtis Drayton or yourself about the price

10 of drugs or money or anything of that nature, correct?

11 A. Correct.

12 Q. Now the first occasion we talked about, it was just you

13 and Curtis Drayton in the car, right?

14 A. Right.

15 Q. No one else?

16 A. Right.

17 Q. And Curtis Drayton didn't know you had a body mike on,

18 did he?

19 A. He did not.

20 Q. On the second occasion, January the 8th, 1993, when you

21 say you went in and saw him, was this in his little

22 cubbyhole office at Central Alabama?

23 A. I don't recall.

24 Q. Do you recall whether or not you all got in an

25 automobile that day?

Chappell Hill testimony transcript, page 88.

1   A. I recall we did not get in an automobile on the second

2   time.

3   Q. But you can't tell us on January 8th, 1993 where you all

4   were when you talked that resulted in the transcript of this

5   body mike recording?

6   A. January the 8th was the third buy.

7   Q. Excuse me. December 28th.

8   A. On December 28th, we were in the office. I do not know

9   which room.

10 Q. All right. Who else was in the office with you and

11 Mr. Drayton?

12 A. I don't recall.

13 Q. Do you recall anybody being there?

14 A. I don't recall. It was two years ago, so --

15 Q. All right. Let's go to January the 8th of 1993, the

16 third.

17 A. Okay.

18 Q. You didn't see your car searched, similar search of your

19 body. You went up to Central Alabama Auto Brokers on

20 January the 8th, '93, correct?

21 A. Correct.

22 Q. All right. What happened when you got there, Mr. Hill?

23 A. I believe there was someone in the parking lot that I

24 spoke to. And shortly thereafter, he entered my car, and I

25 returned to my car.

Chappell Hill testimony transcript, page 89.

1   And we left there and went to Davis Watch Shoppe.

2   Q. And Davis Watch Shoppe is located over on Fairview

3   Avenue, correct?

4   A. Correct.

5   Q. And that would take you in the automobile approximately

6   seven or eight minutes, maybe less --

7   A. Right.

8   Q. -- if you had gone the back way.

9   A. Correct.

10 Q. And you drove over there. And did he get out and go

11 into Davis Watch Shoppe?

12 A. He did.

13 Q. And he got back in the car and then you drove back to

14 Central Alabama Auto Brokers, correct?

15 A. That's correct.

16 Q. And do you remember whether or not on that day anyone

17 was following you, such as Marshall Simons?

18 A. I saw their car when we were crossing through a four-way

19 stop on the way over there. But nobody was right on my

20 tail.

21 Q. All right. And on this occasion, were you in the same

22 vehicle that you were in on the first occasion?

23 A. I believe I was in that same car every time. I was.

24 Q. And have you reviewed the transcript of January the 8th,

25 1993 of -- that was made as a result of the body mike you

Chappell Hill testimony transcript, page 90.

1 were wearing while you and Mr. Drayton went over to the

2 watch shop for him to drop something off and go back to

3 Central Alabama Auto Brokers?

4 A. Yes, I have.

5 Q. And in that recording -- well, first of all, was anyone

6 else in the car with you besides Mr. Drayton?

7 A. No.

8 Q. Once again, just the two of you?

9 A. Correct.

10 Q. Is there any mention in that transcript about drugs?

11 A. No, there is not.

12 Q. Is there any mention in that transcript about the

13 payment of money or how much the drugs are going to cost?

14 A. No, there is not.

15 Q. When you were approached in Tuscaloosa after the fellow

16 went back and got the cocaine out of your drawer at your

17 direction to sell for you and the police approached you,

18 Mr. Hill, it was a pretty scary situation, wasn't it?

19 A. Yes, it was.

20 Q. Here you were in college working on your master's

21 degree, correct?

22 A. Correct.

23 Q. And your business is business, isn't it, Mr. Hill?

24 A. Correct.

25 Q. And not only did you get a degree in business, but you

Chappell Hill testimony transcript, page 91.

1 do business every day; do you not?

2 A. That's correct.

3 Q. And it was very frightening.

4 A. Definitely.

5 Q. You saw it all going down hill, didn't you?

6 A. Yes, I did.

7 Q. Down the drain, correct?

8 A. Correct.

9 Q. And you were very desperate at that time, weren't you,

10 Mr. Hill?

11 A. You could say that.

12 Q. And you can see a desperate situation when you see one,

13 can't you? You recognize it when it's coming, don't you?

14 A. Yes.

15 Q. You're an educated man, correct?

16 A. Correct.

17 Q. And when you were told you've got to make three buys of

18 cocaine from Curtis Drayton, you knew right then what the

19 program was, didn't you?

20 A. Pardon me?

21 Q. It's pretty simple. You knew what the program was,

22 didn't you?

23 A. I knew what I was told to do.

24 Q. You knew what you were told to do.

25   You also knew that if you didn't produce the cocaine on

Chappell Hill testimony transcript, page 92.

1   three sales that you didn't have an agreement that the

2   Government was going to live up to, didn't you, Mr. Hill?

3   You knew that.

4   A. That's correct.

5   Q. And there is no mention of drugs on this body wire, no

6   mention of money on this body wire, on all three occasions,

7   correct?

8   A. Correct.

9   MR. WISE: Your Honor, that's all I have at this

10 time. I would like him subject to recall.

11   THE COURT: Okay. Any other questions?

12   MR. FERNANDEZ: Your Honor, I have two questions.

13 Can I do it from here?

14   THE COURT: Yes.

15   CROSS EXAMINATION

16 BY MR. FERNANDEZ:

17 Q. Mr. Hill, what is your dad's name?

18   THE WITNESS: Is it necessary that I reveal my

19 father's name?

20   THE COURT: Yes.

21   THE WITNESS: Bowen Hill.

22 BY MR. FERNANDEZ:

23 Q. Is he not, Mr. Hill, a prominent attorney in this

24 community?

25 A. It is.

Chappell Hill testimony transcript, page 93.

1   Q. What is your brother's name?

2   A. Mason Hill.

3   Q. Where did Mason Hill work while you were doing all this?

4   A. He worked at the business with Curtis.

5   Q. What business?

6   A. Central Alabama Auto Brokers.

7   Q. He worked in Mr. Drayton's business?

8   A. He worked with Curtis.

9   Q. Did he ever get charged with anything?

10   A. No, he did not.

11   MR. FERNANDEZ: Thank you.

12   THE COURT: Anything else?

13   MR. TESCHNER: Your Honor, if I may just ask a

14 couple of questions.

15   THE COURT: All right.

16   REDIRECT EXAMINATION

17 BY MR. TESCHNER:

18   Q. Mr. Hill, is Curtis Drayton present in the courtroom

19 today?

20   A. Yes, he is.

21   Q. Could you point him out, please, by his location and his

22 apparel?

23   A. He's over there behind Mr. Wise to the right.

24   MR. TESCHNER: If the record may reflect an

25 accurate identification of Mr. Drayton.

Chappell Hill testimony transcript, page 94.

1   MR. WISE: That's correct, Your Honor.

2   THE COURT: All right.

3   BY MR. TESCHNER:

4   Q. Were the tapes that you made with Mr. Drayton at the

5   time of the exchange the only recorded conversations that

6   you had?

7   A. Other than the ones when we were setting up the time to

8   meet.

9   Q. Do you recall generally what you discussed with

10   Mr. Drayton when you were setting up the meetings?

11   A. Could you repeat that? I'm sorry.

12   Q. Do you recall what the conversation was with Mr. Drayton

13   when you set up these meetings?

14   A. That we would meet sometime after lunch.

15   Q. Was it to purchase at car?

16   A. No, it was not.

17   Q. Could you tell the jury what the arrangement was?

18   A. The arrangement was I was going to meet him at the car

19   lot to make the exchange.

20   Q. Well, did he indicate what you were going to get from

21   him?

22   A. I don't recall.

23   MR. TESCHNER: Thank you.

24   Nothing further, Your Honor.

25   THE COURT: All right. You may stand down.

Chappell Hill testimony transcript, page 95.

LAW OFFICES OF

COPELAND, FRANCO, SCREWS & GILL, P. A.

PROFESSIONAL ASSOCIATION

444 SOUTH PERRY STREET

MONTGOMERY, ALABAMA 36104

MAILING ADDRESS:

P. O. BOX 347

MONTGOMERY, AL 36101-0347

HERMAN B. FRANCO
EUEL A. SCREWS, JR.
RICHARD H. GILL
C. LANIER BRANCH
ROBERT D. SEGALL
JOHN A. HENIG, JR.
JAMES M. EDWARDS
E. TERRY BROWN
J. FAIRLEY McDONALD, III

TELEPHONE (334) 834-1180

FACSIMILE (334) 834-3172

LEE H. COPELAND
TRUMAN M. HOBBS, JR.
DAN W. TALIAFERRO
GEORGE W. WALKER, III
PAUL W. COPELAND
ALBERT W. COPELAND
(1927-1983)
DEXTER C. HOBBS
(1956-1990)

October 24, 1995

Mr. Richard Q. Thomas
163 North Haardt Drive
Montgomery, Alabama 36105

      RE: **United States of America v. $30,000**
            Our File No. 2974.001

Dear Squirrel:

    Enclosed is a copy of the signed Stipulation for Compromise
Settlement in the above matter.

                    Sincerely yours,

                    Euel A. Screws, Jr.

EASjr/rtc
Enclosure

Stipulation for compromise settlement.

IN THE UNITED STATES DISTRICT COURT FOR
THE MIDDLE DISTRICT OF ALABAMA
NORTHERN DIVISION

UNITED STATES OF AMERICA,	)	
Plaintiff,	)	
v.	)	CIVIL ACTION NO. 94-M-1008-N
THIRTY THOUSAND DOLLARS ($30,000.00) IN UNITED STATES CURRENCY,	)	
Defendant.	)	

<u>STIPULATION FOR COMPROMISE SETTLEMENT</u>

It is hereby stipulated by and between Plaintiff United States of America (United States), on the one hand, and Claimant Richard Thomas (Thomas), on the other, by and through their respective attorneys, as follows:

1.   That the parties do hereby agree to settle and compromise the above-entitled action upon the terms indicated below.

2.   That Claimant Thomas agrees to the forfeiture of Two Thousand Dollars ($2,000.00) of the Defendant currency to the United States.

3.   The Plaintiff United States and Claimant Thomas agree that Seven Thousand Thirty and 80/100 Dollars ($7,030.80) of the Defendant currency is to be paid to the Clerk of the Court for the Middle District of Alabama to satisfy the balance of the fine assessed against Claimant Thomas in Criminal No. 94-62-N. Claimant Thomas has heretofore paid to the clerk $10,000.00 of the fine assessed against him in Criminal No. 94-62-N.

Settlement stipulation, page 1.

4. That Plaintiff United States and Claimant Thomas agree that the remaining Twenty Thousand Nine Hundred Seventy-Seven Dollars ($20,969.20) of the Defendant currency is to be released to Euel A. Screws, Jr., the attorney representing Claimant Thomas.

5. That Claimant Thomas hereby releases and forever discharges the United States, the State of Alabama, and the City of Montgomery, Alabama, their officers, agents, servants and employees, their successors or assigns, from any and all actions, causes of action, suits, proceedings, debts, dues, contracts, judgments, damages, claims, and/or demands whatsoever in law or equity which Claimant, his heirs, successors, or assigns ever had, now have, or may have in the future in connection with the seizure, detention, and release of the Defendant currency.

A proposed Order is submitted herewith.

FOR THE UNITED STATES ATTORNEY
REDDING PITT

Date: 10/20/95

John T. Harmon
Assistant United States Attorney
Attorney for Plaintiff
United States of America

Date: 10/20/95

Euel A. Screws, Jr.
Attorney for Claimant
Richard Thomas

2

(334) 223-7280
FAX 223-7560

For Claimant: Richard Thomas

Copeland, Franco, Screws & Gill, P.A.
444 South Perry Street (36104)
P.O. Box 347
Montgomery, L 36101-0347
(334) 834-1180

Settlement stipulation, page 2.

UNITED STATES DISTRICT COURT
MIDDLE DISTRICT OF ALABAMA
NORTHERN DIVISION

UNITED STATES OF AMERICA,   :   Case No. 95-202-N
                                   :
          Plaintiff,   :
                                   :
vs.   :
                                   :
MELVIN STARKS,   :
HOWARD ROLLINS,   :
CECIL RHODES,   :
CHARLES HUNDLEY,   :
EDDIE LYONS,   :
RODNEY JEROME TALLEY,   :
GERALD TALLEY,   :
CARZELL TYLER,   :
ERIC QUIN DICKERSON,   :
DWIGHT SWEENEY,   :
WILLIE DEWHART, and   :
CHARLES COLES,   :
                                   :   Montgomery, Alabama
          Defendants.   :   July 20, 1996
                                   :

VOLUME 6
TRIAL TESTIMONY
BEFORE THE HONORABLE ANTHONY A. ALAIMO
United States District Judge and a Jury

Reported By: Norma Hatfield
                          Official Court Reporter
                          801 Gloucester Street, Room 237
                          Post Office Box 1316
                          Brunswick, Georgia 31521-1316
                          (912) 262-9989   FAX (912) 262-9100
                          normah@thebest.net

Trial document, 1996.

1 A. That's correct.

2 Q. Do you know where that card came from?

3 A. Just from where she said it did.

4 Q. Where?

5 A. It was seized from the Lexus. I'm sorry.

6 Q. From whose -Lexus?

7 A. I'm assume it's Curtis Drayton's Lexus.

8 Q. Now with respect to the exhibit, the cloned pager.

9   MR. TESCHNER: Excuse me. May I approach

10 Ms. James, Your Honor?

11 BY MR. TESCHNER:

12 Q. This has been introduced as Starks 86.

13   Could you describe for the jury what period of time

14 calls or pager calls or pager numbers were intercepted, from

15 what date to what date?

16 A. October, '92 -- excuse me -- October, '92 to December,

17 '92.

18 Q. Now the names that were listed as having subscribed to

19 the telephone numbers in the directory or the intercept log,

20 does that include individuals who have been named and

21 convicted in previous indictments?

22 A. Yes, it does.

23 Q. Can you tell the jury, as an investigative tool, was any

24 further use made of the information developed from the

25 cloned pager?

Testimony transcript.

1   A. I'm sorry. In what respect, Mr. Teschner?

2   Q. To establish probable cause to take any other action.

3   A. Yes, sir. This was used as part of the basis for the

4   affidavit for the wiretap.

5   Q. Now if you refer to 2-E1, the notebook that I think you

6   have testified to before, were you able to arrive at any

7   total amounts, at least, reflected in those records of

8   payments made over the course of that year by Mr. Melvin

9   Starks?

10   A. Yes, I did.

11   Q. And what would be the total amount?

12   A. Four hundred and one thousand.

13   Q. Were you able to determine how many kilograms of cocaine

14   were recorded in that book as being distributed to

15   Mr. Melvin Starks?

16   A. Thirteen.

17   Q. Now you referenced, I think, on cross examination some

18   records related to Butch and Duke regarding smaller

19   payments?

20   A. To Butch.

21   Q. To Butch. Would you look through that book, is there

22   only one reference to a person named Butch in various

23   payments in the drug records?

24   A. No. There are several references to Butch, small

25   amounts of money.

Testimony transcript.

REPORT OF INVESTIGATION
(Continuation)

1. FILE NO.	2. G·DEP IDENTIFIER
GO-02-2001	KM2-C1

3. FILE TITLE

Derrick BRADFORD

4. Page 2 of 4

5. PROGRAM CODE

6. DATE PREPARED

7-26-92

stated that DRAYTON used a light green Jaguar registered to Central Alabama Auto Brokers. Thomas GROVE stated that, on one occasion, he met Curtis DRAYTON at Central Alabama Auto Brokers on Carter Hill Road at approximately 7:00 a.m. sometime in September 1991. GROVE stated that Curtis DRAYTON showed him seven or eight kilograms in the trunk of the four-door light green Jaguar while he was at Central Alabama Auto Brokers. GROVE stated that later that same day DRAYTON "fronted" approximately three kilograms of cocaine to Thomas GROVE. GROVE stated that DRAYTON delivered the cocaine on that occasion in a burgundy colored Toyota Cressida. GROVE stated that DRAYTON has delivered kilogram quantities of cocaine in a black Mercedes. Thomas GROVE stated that the profit that DRAYTON makes from cocaine distribution is sent somewhere outside the Montgomery area. GROVE stated further that DRAYTON uses a house on Vaughn Road in Montgomery, Alabama, where he has a girlfriend. GROVE stated that DRAYTON uses the house on Vaughn Road to store large amounts of currency. Thomas GROVE stated that he accompanied Curtis DRAYTON at least twenty times to the residence and assisted DRAYTON in storing the currency in various locations in the residence. GROVE stated that DRAYTON would wrap the money in $10,000.00 bundles and further wrap the currency in tape. Thomas GROVE stated that Curtis DRAYTON has an apartment that he maintains at Vaughn Lakes Apartments. Thomas GROVE stated that he and Curtis DRAYTON had a disagreement over a stolen kilogram of cocaine out of one of Thomas GROVE's apartments in late 1991.

3. Thomas GROVE stated that, when he received kilogram quantities of cocaine from DRAYTON, they would be in the form that they were smuggled in. GROVE stated that they would not be cut and the kilograms would have original wrappings on them. GROVE stated that the original wrappings included plastic and would be contained in a box used for wrapping presents. GROVE stated that a karate figure would be painted or a type of sticker affixed to the plastic wrappings on the kilograms of cocaine. GROVE stated that many of the kilograms of cocaine would come in a green present box and inside the box would be grey paper on top of clear plastic. GROVE stated that Curtis DRAYTON always had uncut cocaine. Thomas GROVE stated that Lorenzo HUGHES is Curtis DRAYTON's "right hand man" and has been present with Lorenzo HUGHES at the Vaughn Road residence. Thomas GROVE stated that Lorenzo HUGHES distributes ounce quantities of cocaine and usually distributes approximately one kilogram weekly and distributes approximately two to three kilograms of cocaine on a consignment basis to other people in large quantities. GROVE stated that a Cedric "LNU" works for Curtis DRAYTON and distributes in Trenholm Court.

4. Thomas GROVE stated that the pound of cocaine that was recovered in the Chevrolet Blazer that Derrick BRADFORD was driving was his. Thomas GROVE stated that he had placed an order with Derrick BRADFORD approximately four days before the seizure occurred. (A pound of cocaine was recovered from Derrick BRADFORD on 4-21-92 and BRADFORD was later arrested.) GROVE stated that he had paged BRADFORD on 4-21-92 in order to obtain his cocaine. Thomas GROVE stated that Mason HILL works with Curtis DRAYTON and is knowledgeable about DRAYTON's activities. GROVE stated that Mason HILL from time to time will receive approximately one-half kilogram of cocaine and distribute it to persons that

DEA Form — 6a
(May 1980)

EXH # 9
1 OF 2

Government's chief witness, Thomas Grove's testimony.

IN THE UNITED STATES DISTRICT COURT FOR
THE MIDDLE DISTRICT OF ALABAMA
NORTHERN DIVISION

UNITED STATES OF AMERICA,	)	
	)	
Plaintiff,	)	
	)	
v.	)	CIVIL ACTION NO. 94-M-1008-N
	)	
THIRTY THOUSAND DOLLARS	)	
($30,000.00) IN UNITED STATES	)	
CURRENCY,	)	
	)	
Defendant.	)	

ORDER

Based on the foregoing Stipulation for Compromise Settlement, it is hereby ORDERED AND ADJUDGED:

1. That Two Thousand Dollars ($2,000.00) of the Defendant currency is hereby forfeited to the United States of America to be disposed of according to law;

2. That Seven Thousand Thirty and 80/100 Dollars ($7,030.80) of the Defendant currency is to be paid forthwith to the Clerk of the Court for the Middle District of Alabama to satisfy the balance of the fine assessed against Claimant Thomas in Criminal No. 94-62-N;

3. That the United States Marshal forthwith release Twenty Thousand Nine Hundred Seventy-Seven Dollars ($20,969.20) to Euel A. Screws, Jr., the attorney representing Claimant Thomas; and

4. That a copy of this Order be furnished to the United States Marshal.

SO ORDERED, this _____ day of October, 1995.

_____
UNITED STATES MAGISTRATE JUDGE

Screws's $2,000 forfeiture.

Index